REVISE EDEXCEL GCSE

Physical Education
Unit 1 Theory of PE (5PE01 & 5PE03)

REVISION WORKBOOK

Series Consultant: Harry Smith   Author: Jan Simister

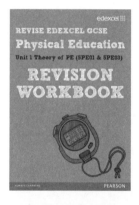

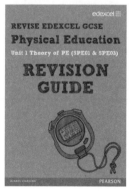

THE REVISE EDEXCEL SERIES
Available in print or online

Online editions for all titles in the Revise Edexcel series are available Autumn 2012.

Presented on our ActiveLearn platform, you can view the full book and customise it by adding notes, comments and weblinks.

Print editions

PE Revision Workbook	9781446903636
PE Revision Guide	9781446903629

Online editions

PE Revision Workbook	9781446903674
PE Revision Guide	9781446903650

This Revision Workbook is designed to complement your classroom and home learning, and to help prepare you for the exam. It does not include all the content and skills needed for the complete course. It is designed to work in combination with Edexcel's main GCSE Physical Education 2009 Series.

D1354257

To find out more visit:
www.pearsonschools.co.uk/edexcelgcsePErevision

Contents

This book covers the content for both the full course and short course.

A small bit of small print
Edexcel publishes Sample Assessment Material and the Specification on its website. This is the official content and this book should be used in conjunction with it. The questions in this book have been written to help you practise what you have learned in your revision. Remember: the real exam questions may not look like this.

Target grades
Target grades are quoted in this book for some of the questions. Students targeting this grade should be aiming to get most of the marks available. Students targeting a higher grade should be aiming to get all of the marks available.

Health and physical activity

 1 Year 9 students who regularly attended team practices in school were asked why they took part in physical activity.

Complete the table below by stating the category of each of their answers. **(3 marks)**

Reasons for taking part in physical activity	Category (State whether this is a mental, physical or social benefit)
I go because my friends go	Social
My doctor said I was overweight	Physical
I enjoy it	Mental

 2 In order to achieve a healthy active lifestyle, an individual needs to consider several different factors. Which of the following statements **best** describes a healthy active lifestyle?

(1 mark)

☐ **A** Playing sport and training twice a week

☒ **B** Walking 20 minutes each day and eating a balanced diet

☐ **C** Making sure there is opportunity for recovery after activity and eating a balanced diet

☐ **D** Playing in a football match

> Remember to highlight key words in questions to help you.

 3 The image below shows performers participating in a bowls match.

> Make sure you follow the instruction to give two different reasons. Give two different categories of answer.

Over 40s bowls team

Give **two** different reasons why the over 40s bowls players may take part in physical activity. **(2 marks)**

So that they keep their muscles and bones moving so they don't go stiff and so they can make friends of a similar age and interests as them.

> Remember to apply your answer to the activity in the picture.

1

Mental benefits of an active lifestyle

G 1 Which of the following is considered to be a **mental** benefit of exercise?   **(1 mark)**

☐ **A** Working in a team

☐ **B** Developing friendships

☒ **C** Competition

☐ **D** Improved coordination

> Check your category and look out for similar words.

C 2 Membership of a sporting club is said to stimulate competition. Outline how being a member of a local football club would give a player the opportunity to be competitive.

(1 mark)

A local football club could play matches

against other teams.

F 3 Complete the statements below about the benefits gained from participating in physical activity.

> **Guided**

(a) Many people take part in physical activity to ....relieve.... stress. This is a

............................mental............................ benefit of physical activity.

(2 marks)

C (b) People who take part in physical activity, especially activities such as gymnastics and dance, can gain an ....Aesthetic........................ appreciation of the activity, due to the quality of the movements being performed.

(1 mark)

C (c) People who participate in physical activity regularly are often disappointed when they cannot train. One possible reason for this is that the body doesn't release or manufacture as much ....serotonin.......................... as it would normally release as a result of physical activity. The presence of this chemical in the brain accounts for the ....feel good.................... factor experienced by performers.

(2 marks)

Mental and physical benefits

 1 Complete the table below by stating **three** reasons why people may join a sports club. Make sure your reason matches the category given in the table.   **(3 marks)**

Reason for joining a sports club	Category
1 To release stress	Mental
2 To get competative	Mental
3 To lose weight to gain confidance.	Mental **and** physical

 2 The box below identifies a number of the benefits of exercise. Although some of these statements indicate a physical benefit, these could also lead to mental health benefits.

Identify **two physical** benefits from the box and state how these **physical** benefits could lead to improvement in **mental** health.

> I enjoy competition.
>
> It can lead to weight loss, which is good if you are overweight. + gain confidance
>
> It can improve fitness.
>
> It makes me feel less tense.
>
> It gives me greater muscle definition.
>
> It can improve self-esteem.
>
> It can improve my physical health.

> Always read the introduction. It will lead you in to the question. Note the two requirements: *identify* and *state how*.

Physical benefit 1:   **(1 mark)**

If can lead to weightloss, which is good if you're overweight.

How physical benefit improves mental health: **(1 mark)**

> **Guided**

Can improve self-esteem if you are happier with your healthier weight.

Physical benefit 2:   **(1 mark)**

If gives me greater muscle definition

How physical benefit improves mental health: **(1 mark)**

Have a better looking body

EXAM ALERT

If you are asked to relate one answer to another, make sure that you do. In this case, you need to link a mental benefit to the physical benefit you have selected. If you cannot think of a mental benefit, choose a different option from the list!

Students have struggled with exam questions similar to this – **be prepared!**   ResultsPlus

Fitness benefits of an active lifestyle

E 1 Give **one** possible reason why each of the following people may participate in sport.

> Note that these questions require reasons, not categories.

(a) Graham's mum has noticed she is gaining a lot of weight, putting her at risk of becoming overfat. **(1 mark)**

So that she can lose weight so she's not unhealthy

C (b) John has recently grown very tall. He has become conscious of how thin he is and has decided to go to the local gym. **(1 mark)**

So he can gain muscle changing his physical appearance which can help him gain confidence and better self esteem.

A 2 The performers in the image below train regularly to improve their performance in table tennis.

Table tennis training

> Don't forget to relate your answer to the activity in the picture.

Describe **two** of the possible physical fitness benefits for the performers if they train regularly. **(4 marks)**

Guided

One fitness benefit of taking part in regular exercise is an improvement in cardiovascular fitness. This is due to *you increasing your stamina levels but also building muscle which means they can work for longer improves muscular endurance in legs and arms meaning there will be an improved performance in the match(s)*

Health benefits of an active lifestyle

1 The image shows an individual participating in sport.

> Note that these questions are about physical **health**, not physical fitness.

(a) Identify **two** different physical health benefits the tennis player may gain through participation in physical activity. **(2 marks)**

Greater muscle definition due to repeatedly practising the same skills and using the same muscles. Losing weight if overweight is also another physical benefit because your body will be healthier than it was before you started playing tennis.

> Watch out for words like 'different'. When you see them, make sure you give a broad range of answers. In this case, give examples from two different body systems.

> Students have struggled with exam questions similar to this – **be prepared!** ResultsPlus

(b) Describe how the physical health benefits you identified in (a) can be achieved.

(4 marks)

Weightloss can be achieved by burning excess calories by playing sports which can prevent weight gain. Also using the same muscles could build tone and definition.

Social benefits of an active lifestyle

D 1 George is 16 years old. Although he has always enjoyed PE, he is very shy.

Complete the table below by explaining how, through joining a sports club, George may achieve **two** different types of benefit. **(4 marks)**

	Benefit	How achieved
1	Social – making new friends (1)	By joining a club, he will meet new people and can make friends with them (1)
2	improving cooperation skills by working as a team. (1)	working in a team (1)

Guided

C 2 The children in the image below are playing 10-pin bowling. Explain how participation in a physical activity such as 10-pin bowling can improve social health. **(2 marks)**

It is a team game where team players need to work together by communicating with each other. They could also make friends with some of their team mates.

D 3 Desmond enjoyed athletics and swimming and would often run or swim in his free time.

Explain how Desmond could use participation in these activities to improve his social health **(3 marks)**

He could go swimming with his friends or run with a partner so they can improve together. He could also join a swimming or running club where he could meet new people and make friends.

Had a go ☐   Nearly there ☐   Nailed it! ☐

Key influences: people

E 1 'Family' is an example taken from the 'people' category of key influences on participation in physical activity. Give **three** examples from 'family' that might impact on participation.

(3 marks)

Family family act as role models

Brothers and sisters could influence each

other and participate together.

Distant family could inspire and act as

role models or show family sporting traditions

D 2 Which people are the **key** influences acting on Luke in the following paragraph?

Luke really enjoys going to the tennis club but is <u>under pressure from some of his friends to give it up</u> as they prefer to spend time in the library at lunch times. He isn't sure what to do, <u>as his mum has just bought him a new racket for his birthday and has paid for him to join a club outside school</u>. <u>Both Luke's sisters already play tennis to a good standard and he wants to be good enough to play against them</u>. **(3 marks)**

> Circle or underline key words in the question that will help you to identify key influences.

Lukes friends want him to be sociable

with them

sisters are role models

His mum encourage him

C 3 There are many key influences that impact on whether we choose to participate in physical activity or not. Identify the key influences that could impact on us in the following situations:

(3 marks)

(a) When reading the 'sports' section of a newspaper. *role models*

(b) Going to a 'taster session' for rugby as someone in your class recommended it. *peers*

(c) Playing tennis at a local club where your mum and sisters are members. *family*

Role models in the paper

Friends recommended it

Family club members

Key influences: image

G

1 Table 1 identifies examples of key influences that can impact on our ability to achieve sustained involvement in physical activity

Identify **two** key influences belonging to the 'Image' category. **(2 marks)**

Table 1

Peers	Radio
Status	Sports channels on satellite television
Friends	Family

Status and Radio

Sports channels on satellite television

C

2 The key influences media coverage and fashion have impacted on some of the students in the following extract.

Identify the statement in the extract where these key influences are impacting on the students on their school ski trip. **(2 marks)**

Extract

The ski party left school at 5 am, many parents were there to see their children off on the trip, many parents themselves skiers. Several of the students had family members with them on the trip, either older or younger siblings. Although all of the students didn't know each other at the start of the trip they soon became friends whilst away. There was a choice between skiing or snowboarding, most of the group opted for snowboarding as they thought it was more modern. Whilst away there was opportunity to watch competition downhill skiing on the television, after seeing the excitement of the event and it being broadcast on every channel some of the students changed from snowboarding to skiing.

Seeing participants on TV could make them want to try something new as they have not seen snowboarding in action. They thought snowboarding was more modern and broadcast on TV

G

3 Which of the following is **not** a media coverage key influence? **(1 mark)**

☐ **A** Commentator on the radio

☒ **B** Presentation in school

☐ **C** Newspaper article

☐ **D** TV programme

Had a go ☐   Nearly there ☐   Nailed it! ☐

Key influences: culture

D 1 Identify the key influences that could impact on us in the following situations:

(a) Mike plays competitive rugby but will be 50 next year and thinks that by then he will take up a physically less demanding sport. **(1 mark)**

.....*Age*..

(b) Millie really enjoyed participating in sport. But outside of school she had a limited choice of places to play basketball as few venues in her local area catered for visually impaired performers. **(1 mark)**

.....*Resources   for   disabled   players*...

(c) Rebecca loved participating in boxing and went to the local club with her brothers. Of the 40 boxers registered at the club Rebecca was the only female. **(1 mark)**

.....*Gender*..

C 2 The table below identifies examples of key influences that can impact on our ability to achieve sustained involvement in physical activity.

Use the key influences in the table below to complete the statements below about cultural key influences.

Do not use any key influence more than once in your answers. **(4 marks)**

Table 1

Peers	Media
Age	Access
Illness	Disability
Role models	Gender
Race	Status of activity

(a) ....*Race / Age*......................... is an example of a cultural key influence.

(b) Participation can be limited due to a lack of availability of adapted sports. This is an

example of an impact due to ......*Disability*................................. .

(c) Stereotyping can result in some people being pushed towards one sport rather than

another, due to their ....*Race*.................................. . This is a cultural

key influence.

(d) Some girls will not take part in some activities that have traditionally been

considered 'boys' sports. This is a ....*Gender*.............................cultural

key influence.

Key influences: resources

　1　The following extract is from a statement made by Dave when asked why he no longer plays sport.

'Well, I have a full-time job and have to leave the house at 7 in the morning to get to work on time. There's a gym in the building where I work but the boss doesn't allow us to take a longer lunch break, which I'd need so I can shower afterwards. I leave work at 6 pm and when I get home there's so much to do with the family that I can't exercise then either.'

What key influence in the 'Resource' category is Dave using to justify not participating in physical activity?　**(1 mark)**

Time

EXAM ALERT

Look for key information in the scenario. There is a lot of text in the question and it is designed to help you. What examples of the resource category of key influences do you know? Are any of them mentioned in the scenario?

Exam questions similar to this have proved especially tricky in the past – **be prepared!**　ResultsPlus

　2　Complete the statements below to identify the key influences impacting on sustained involvement in physical activity.

(a)　Eve wanted to play golf but it cost too much to play at the local country club.　**(1 mark)**

Access

(b)　Greg can only use the pool when the hoist is operating to lower him in and then lift him out when he has finished his session.　**(1 mark)**

Access

(c)　Joyce went skiing with the school and would love to continue skiing but she doesn't live near enough to a dry ski slope.　**(1 mark)**

Location

(d)　Kam used to play a lot of netball whilst at school but since leaving school she has stopped playing as she cannot find a netball club in her local area.　**(1 mark)**

Availability

Key influences: health and wellbeing and socio-economic

C

1   The statements in the extract below were made by a variety of participants when asked why they played the sports they did. The key influences impact on achieving sustained involvement in physical activity.

Identify the statements relating to the key influences **health and wellbeing** and **socio-economic.**   **(3 marks)**

Extract

Roger plays table tennis, he used to play tennis but found since his operation he could no longer cover the court so decided to play something that meant he didn't need to move around as much. Roger has also thought about playing golf because he liked the status of the activity, but there are no golf clubs near to where he lives. Abena says she likes to play badminton on a regular basis to keep fit and give her the chance to meet up with her friends, although she admitted she had missed the last four sessions due to a very bad cold. Paul used to horse ride once a week but now he is older his parents have stopped paying for him and he cannot afford the fees.

....

....

....

....

....

....

D

2   There are socio-economic key influences that impact on our choice of physical activity.

Which of the following is an example of a socio-economic key influence?   **(1 mark)**

  ☐ **A**   I play football because I want to be as well-known as David Beckham

  ☐ **B**   I go horse riding because all of my friends do

  ☒ **C**   How people see me is important to me and my business – that's why I play golf at the country club

  ☐ **D**   I play tennis because the club is easy to get to

C

3   The following activities have been ranked in order of number of people participating. Identify the key influence that could result in this rank order of 'popularity'.

1	Basketball at school lunch time club	**4**	Swimming at the local leisure centre
2	Football in the park with friends	**5**	Golf at a private golf club
3	Tennis in the park after school on the free courts	**6**	Horse riding on own pony **(1 mark)**

....

Roles and required qualities

E

Guided

1 Describe **three** types of key quality required to become a successful official. **(3 marks)**

One good quality for an official is to have good knowledge of the sport. Another quality is ...

....

....

....

....

....

G

2 (a) There are a variety of ways in which an individual can become, or remain, involved in physical activity. Officiating is one of the roles; identify **two** others. **(2 marks)**

....

....

B

(b) Explain why it is important to have a choice of available roles in physical activity.

(3 marks)

Guided

To give people options ....

....

....

....

....

....

B

3 For an activity of your choice, explain the range of roles available and how this would allow a variety of people to become involved. **(3 marks)**

Activity:...

....

....

....

....

Sports participation pyramid 1

E   1   State which stage of the sports participation pyramid is being described by the participants in each of the following statements.   **(3 marks)**

   (a) 'I joined a club last month because I enjoyed the introductory sessions so much.'

   ....

   (b) 'It was great; it's the first time I've tried kite-boarding.'

   ....

> Look for the key words. In this case the activity is irrelevant. What matters is 'it's the first time I've tried'. Now you just need to name the stage at which we all start when we try a new activity.

   (c) 'I feel I know a few more of the skills I need to play the game.'

   ....

EXAM ALERT

> Many students fail to name a stage. The question asks for the name of the stage, so descriptions will not be given credit even if correct.

> Students have struggled with exam questions similar to this – **be prepared!**   ResultsPlus

D   2   Describe the foundation stage of the sports participation pyramid.   **(3 marks)**

   ....

   ....

   ....

   ....

   ....

   ....

B   3   Outline how someone could move from the foundation stage to the participation stage of the sports participation pyramid.   **(2 marks)**

   ....

   ....

   ....

   ....

Sports participation pyramid 2

D 1 Identify which stage of the sports participation pyramid is being described by the participants in each of the following statements. **(3 marks)**

(a) 'I've been lucky enough to get some really good coaching recently and I feel my skills have been developed.'

....

(b) 'I've moved up to the first team this season. Next season I hope to move to a better team, so I can continue to improve and start to get noticed by the national selection committee.'

....

(c) 'I really enjoyed the move from playing at county to national level.'

....

C 2 Describe the performance stage of the sports participation pyramid. **(3 marks)**

....

....

....

....

....

....

B 3 Outline what someone needs to do to move from the performance stage to the elite stage of the sports participation pyramid. **(2 marks)**

....

....

....

....

Initiatives and their common purposes

C   1   Initiatives such as the Youth Sport Trust's TOP programme aim to contribute to the development of healthy, active lifestyles.

Outline **two** different ways that initiatives such as this can lead to a healthier, more active lifestyle.   **(2 marks)**

....

....

....

....

A   2   Describe, using examples, how initiatives for becoming or remaining involved in physical activity can contribute to the development of a healthy lifestyle.

> Note: this is an extended answer question so you should write your answers as fully as possible.

(6 marks)

Guided   Initiatives can increase participation ....

....

....

....

....

....

....

....

....

....

....

....

....

Agencies

E   1   Sport England is one agency involved in the provision of opportunities for becoming, or remaining, involved in physical activity. Name **two** other agencies.   **(2 marks)**

....

....

C   2   **(a)**   Identify the agency being described in the extract below.   **(1 mark)**

> **Extract**
>
> This agency uses National Lottery funding and works with UK Sport to deliver a mass participation sporting legacy from the 2012 Olympic Games. Some of their initiatives to increase participation have included 'Places People Play'; their strategy for 2012–17 is 'Creating a Sporting Habit for Life'.

....

    (b)   Identify **one** other agency that will work with the agency you have identified in (a) to achieve their initiatives   **(1 mark)**

....

E   3   The following are all different examples of the same type of agency. Identify the type of agency.   **(1 mark)**

    1   Amateur swimming association

    2   British cycling

    3   British gymnastics

    4   The rugby football union

    5   British volleyball association

    6   The lawn tennis association

....

Health, fitness and exercise

D   1   Give the meanings of the terms 'health' and 'fitness'.   **(2 marks)**

....

....

....

....

EXAM ALERT

> These terms are generally confused with one another. Ensure you learn the definition in the specification glossary.

> Students have struggled with exam questions similar to this – **be prepared!**   **ResultsPlus**

B   2   Using examples, explain what it means to be fit.   **(3 marks)**

Guided

Fitness is ....

Different people will require different levels of fitness depending on ....

....

....

....

....

> Highlight the instructions in questions, so that you don't forget them. For this question you need to give examples and explain a term.

B   3   Explain how exercise links to performance in physical activity.   **(3 marks)**

....

....

....

....

....

....

Health, fitness and exercise and a balanced healthy lifestyle

C 1 Complete the statements below about exercise and fitness as part of a healthy, active lifestyle. **(3 marks)**

(a) .... is a form of physical activity done to maintain or improve health.

(b) Performance should improve with an increase in ....

(c) ...., fitness and exercise all contribute positively to create a balanced, healthy lifestyle.

A 2 **Figure 1** indicates a link between the four terms identified. Describe the link between these terms. **(4 marks)**

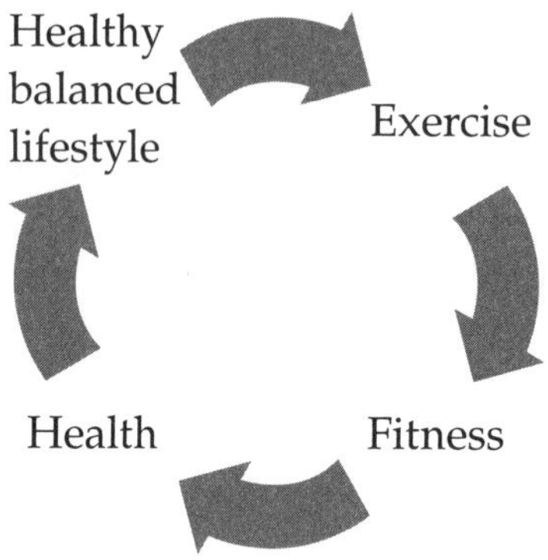

Healthy balanced lifestyle — Exercise — Fitness — Health

Figure 1

Guided

Exercise can lead to increased fitness ....

....

....

....

....

....

....

....

Cardiovascular fitness and muscular endurance

F

1 As a result of adopting an active lifestyle, an individual may improve aspects of health-related exercise. Which of the following gives the best explanation of muscular endurance?

(1 mark)

☐ **A** The ability to exercise the entire body for long periods of time without tiring

☐ **B** The ability to exercise the heart and lungs and muscles in the body for long periods

☐ **C** The ability to exercise the muscles of the body for long periods of time without tiring

☐ **D** The ability to exercise the entire body for long periods of time

D

2 Complete the following statements about cardiovascular fitness and muscular endurance.

(a) Cardiovascular fitness relies on the cardiovascular system supplying sufficient

.... to allow enough energy to be released so that

performers can continue to .... for long periods of

time without ....   **(3 marks)**

(b) To have high levels of muscular endurance, the ....

and lungs must work together to supply sufficient oxygen to the

.... so that they can maintain the

.... of the work they are doing.   **(3 marks)**

(c) A good level of cardiovascular fitness can reduce the chance of suffering from

...., thus

cardiovascular fitness contributes to a balanced healthy lifestyle.   **(1 mark)**

D

3 Explain the difference between muscular endurance and cardiovascular fitness.   **(3 marks)**

....

....

....

....

....

EXAM ALERT

Differentiate clearly between cardiovascular fitness and muscular endurance. Very often, a good way to explain the difference between two things is to add examples to your answer, even if not specifically asked for in the question.

Students have struggled with exam questions similar to this – **be prepared!** ResultsPlus

Muscular strength, flexibility and body composition

1 Match the following definitions to the correct components of health-related exercise by drawing a line to link the definition and component.

Match one definition to one component of health-related exercise. Not all definitions will be used.

(5 marks)

Definitions

| The ability to use voluntary muscles many times without getting tired |

| The ability to exercise the entire body for long periods of time without tiring |

| The ability to change the position of the body quickly and to control the movement of the whole body |

| The ability to use two or more body parts together |

| The amount of force a muscle can exert against a resistance |

| The range of movement possible at a joint |

| The ability to do strength performances quickly |

| The differential rate at which an individual is able to perform a movement or cover a distance in a period of time |

| The percentage of body weight that is fat, muscle and bone |

Components of health-related exercise

| Body composition |

| Flexibility |

| Cardiovascular fitness |

| Muscular strength |

| Muscular endurance |

Agility, balance and coordination

E 1 Coordination is: **(1 mark)**

☐ **A** working together in a team for the benefit of all

☐ **B** how well a task is completed

☐ **C** the ability to change position quickly and with control

☐ **D** the ability to use two or more body parts together

D 2 Complete the following statements.

Guided

(a) .....Agility..... is about changing direction quickly. It is a component of

.... -related ....fitness..... . **(2 marks)**

(b) There are six components of .... -related

.... This component gives the performer the ability

to retain the body's centre of mass above the base of support; the component is called

.... **(2 marks)**

3 Agility and coordination are both components of skill-related fitness.

C (a) Explain the terms agility and coordination. **(2 marks)**

....

....

....

....

B (b) Explain how good coordination aids agility. **(2 marks)**

....

....

....

....

Power, reaction time and speed 1

1 Draw lines to match each of the following definitions to the correct components of skill-related fitness.

Guided

Match one definition to one component of skill-related fitness. Not all definitions will be used.

(6 marks)

Definitions

Components of skill-related fitness

The ability to use voluntary muscles many times without getting tired

The ability to exercise the entire body for long periods of time without tiring

The ability to change the position of the body quickly and to control the movement of the whole body

The ability to use two or more body parts together

The amount of force a muscle can exert against a resistance

The range of movement possible at a joint

The ability to do strength performances quickly

The differential rate at which an individual is able to perform a movement or cover a distance in a period of time

The percentage of body weight that is fat, muscle and bone

The time between the presentation of a stimulus and the onset of a movement

The ability to retain the body's centre of mass (gravity) above the base of support with reference to static (stationary), or dynamic (changing) conditions of movement, shape and orientation

Power

Speed

Reaction time

Coordination

Balance

Agility

Effects of cardiovascular fitness and muscular endurance

E 1 Which of the following statements is **incorrect**?   **(1 mark)**

☐ **A** Long distance runners require good cardiovascular fitness when they complete a sprint finish

☐ **B** Games players are more likely to maintain the quality of their play throughout the match if they have excellent cardiovascular fitness

☐ **C** Muscular endurance is vital in long distance events such as the Tour de France cycle race

☐ **D** Skaters need good muscular endurance to cover the 10,000 m in a long track race

D 2 Complete each of the following statements by using one of the components of health-related exercise.   **(3 marks)**

(a) Giles has an unsuitable level of .... for his activity (long distance running). This makes participation in his activity more difficult due to his inability to get sufficient oxygen around his body and to his working muscles.

(b) Without sufficient ...., Liz would not be able to maintain a good pace throughout the race.

(c) Jason was substituted in the second half as his muscles were too tired to continue to work. Jason will need to work on his .... if he wants to play for the whole game in the future.

C 3 Explain how the tennis player in **Figure 1** uses cardiovascular fitness and muscular endurance in a match.   **(4 marks)**

....

....

....

....

....

> There are four marks available so in total you need to make four points, two for each component.

Figure 1

A 4 Explain why cardiovascular fitness is more important to a marathon runner than speed.   **(3 marks)**

....

....

....

....

....

Effects of muscular strength, flexibility and body composition

E

1   Identify the most relevant component of health-related exercise for a gymnast when performing the splits. **(1 mark)**

☐ **A** Muscular endurance

☐ **B** Cardiovascular fitness

☐ **C** Flexibility

☐ **D** Muscular strength

C

2   Flexibility is an important component of health-related exercise for many activities. Complete the table below to explain how flexibility is used by each performer in their activity. **(3 marks)**

> **Guided**

Performer	How flexibility is used in activity
Sprinter	At the hip to get a long stride length therefore using as few strides as possible to complete the race in a quicker time
Javelin thrower	
Gymnast in a floor routine	

A

3   Evaluate the importance of body composition for a gymnast and games player, giving examples of its possible impact on performance. **(6 marks)**

....

....

....

....

> There will be two extended answer questions in your exam. If a question says 'evaluate' you need to give reasons for and against and include a conclusion.

....

....

....

....

....

....

Effects of agility, balance and coordination

E

1 Which of the following components of fitness is skill-related and the most important for a goalkeeper diving to save a deflected shot on goal. **(1 mark)**

EXAM ALERT

☐ **A** Agility

☐ **B** Power

☐ **C** Muscular strength

☐ **D** Body composition

> The question asks for a component of **skill-related fitness** so you can cross out any options which are health-related.

> Students have struggled with exam questions similar to this – **be prepared!** ResultsPlus

C

2 This question relates to components of skill-related fitness that are used in physical activity to contribute to a balanced healthy lifestyle.

State the component of skill-related fitness being described in each statement:

(a) .... is the ability to change the direction of the body quickly. **(1 mark)**

(b) Squash players need .... to move the racket to the right place to strike the ball correctly. **(1 mark)**

C

3 Give examples to demonstrate the importance of agility in **two** different sporting activities.

Guided

Squash players need agility to change direction quickly to reach the ball ....

....

Footballers need to use agility to ....

(2 marks)

C

4 Give examples to demonstrate the importance of coordination in two different sporting activities. **(2 marks)**

....

....

....

B

5 Explain how the high jumper in **Figure 1** uses balance in her event. **(2 marks)**

....

....

....

....

Figure 1

25

Power, reaction time and speed 2

B

Guided

1   In the table, describe how each performer uses speed and what its effect is on performance.

(6 marks)

Performer	Example of use of speed by performer in activity	Effect of speed on performance
Rugby player	To sprint past opponents with the ball	
Sprinter		To run faster and beat opponents
Long jumper		

C

2   The images show two different participants engaging in exercise and physical activity.

(a) Name **two** components of skill-related fitness that both participants need in order to be successful in their activities.   **(2 marks)**

Component 1:...

Component 2:...

(b) Explain the use of each component for the javelin thrower.   **(2 marks)**

....

....

....

....

PAR-Q and fitness tests

E 1 Help develop the PAR-Q shown below by adding **two** more typical questions that would normally be asked before allowing someone to take part in physical activity. **(2 marks)**

> What health and lifestyle issues might you need to know about before deciding if someone should exercise, or how much they should do?

PAR-Q

Name: Kam Kaur

Address: 21 Upper Street

London

_____

Personal dimensions (weight; height; sex):
9st, 5'6", female

1. Do you currently smoke? Yes / No

2. Do you drink more than recommended maximum
   (21 units for men and 14 units for women)? Yes / No

3. Do you exercise on a regular basis (at least 3 times a week)? Yes / No

4. Have you ever felt pain in your chest when you do physical exercise?
   Yes / No

5. _____

6. _____

7. Do you know of any other reason why you should not participate in a
   programme of physical activity? Yes / No

E 2 The table below shows the ratings from Michael's latest set of fitness tests. If you were Michael's coach, explain how you could use these ratings to improve Michael's training programme. **(3 marks)**

Fitness Test	Rating
Ruler drop test	Average
Sargent jump test	Good
Sit and reach test	Below average
30 m sprint	Good

....

....

....

....

....

Fitness tests 1

D   1   (a)   Describe the Cooper's 12-minute run test.   **(4 marks)**

....

....

....

....

....

....

....

....

B   (b)   Explain why you would use the Cooper's 12-minute run test.   **(3 marks)**

....

....

....

....

....

....

B   2   Explain whether you would use a treadmill test or the Harvard step test to measure the cardiovascular fitness of a group of Year 9 students.   **(3 marks)**

....

....

....

When asked to explain, don't forget to give reasons for your answer. You could start by saying 'I would use the .... because…'

....

....

....

....

Fitness tests 2

1   (a)   Identify the tests shown in Figure 1 and Figure 2.   **(2 marks)**

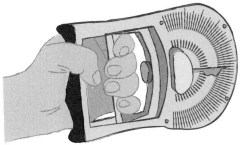   

Figure 1   **Figure 2**

Figure 1: ....

Figure 2: ....

(b)   Name the aspects of fitness being tested in figures 1 and 2.   **(2 marks)**

Figure 1: ....

Figure 2: ....

(c)   Name a sporting activity that you would probably be training for if you used these fitness tests to measure your fitness.

Use a different sporting activity for each test.   **(2 marks)**

Figure 1: ....

Figure 2: ....

(d)   Which of the following statements is correct?   **(1 mark)**

    ☐   **A**   Both tests measure an aspect of health-related exercise

    ☐   **B**   Both tests measure an aspect of skill-related fitness

    ☐   **C**   One of these tests is a test of health-related exercise; the other is a test of skill-related fitness

Fitness tests 3

B 1 (a) Identify **one** way in which the 30-metre sprint test is different from the Illinois agility test. **(1 mark)**

....

....

B (b) Explain how this variation makes the tests more relevant for their particular use.

(2 marks)

....

....

....

....

C (c) (i) Name **two** different activities that would be suitable for an individual who achieved an 'excellent' rating in the 30-metre sprint test. **(2 marks)**

....

....

(ii) For each of these activities explain how speed would be an advantage. **(2 marks)**

....

....

....

....

....

G 2 (a) Name the fitness test shown in the diagram. **(1 mark)**

....

(b) Identify an activity where the performers would find the results of this test useful. **(1 mark)**

....

....

5 M

9.15 M

Fitness tests 4

Figure 1 and **Figure 2** show performers engaged in two different fitness tests.

D 1 (a) Name the test in use in **Figure 1**.   **(1 mark)**

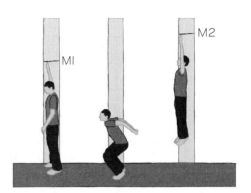

Figure 1   Figure 2

....

(b) Name the test in use in **Figure 2**.   **(1 mark)**

....

(c) Describe the test protocol for the test shown in **Figure 1**.   **(3 marks)**

....

....

....

....

....

....

Fitness tests 5

B 1 The school football team underwent a number of fitness tests before starting on a training programme. The results for the reaction time test for six members of the team are shown in **Table 1**.

Table 1

Student	Reaction time test result
A	28 cm
B	16 cm
C	9 cm
D	25 cm
E	10 cm
F	8 cm

> Remember, a low score for reaction time is better than a high score!

(a) Name a reaction time test. **(1 mark)**

....

(b) Using the data in **Table 1**, explain which student you would choose to play as goalkeeper. **(4 marks)**

....

....

....

....

....

....

B 2 Explain whether the following tests would be relevant to measure the school swimming team's fitness for their activity. **(3 marks)**

Standing stork test	Ruler drop test	Three ball juggle

....

....

....

....

....

Principles of training: progressive overload

(A) 1 (a) Explain how you could tell if progressive overload was being applied in a training programme. **(3 marks)**

....

....

....

....

....

....

(B) (b) Explain how you could tell if progressive overload had been successfully applied in a training programme by looking at an individual's fitness test results. **(4 marks)**

Guided

If I looked at the results of the first set of tests and compared these to the second, I

would see that ....

....

....

....

....

(C) 2 Identify the statement that shows the principle of progressive overload is being applied. **(1 mark)**

☐ **A** I trained for a few weeks before increasing the amount I lifted and I was careful to only increase it slowly so that I didn't get injured

☐ **B** A friend of mine waited a week before they increased the workload, then they went from 15 kg to 30 kg in one go

☐ **C** After the injury I couldn't workout at all for 4 weeks

☐ **D** The following list shows the amounts I lifted on a week-by-week basis: 5 kg; 6 kg; 7 kg; 8 kg; 7 kg

Principles of training: specificity

D 1 The performers listed below all apply the principles of training to their training programmes. Name the training method these performers would be most likely to use if applying the principle of specificity to their training. **(4 marks)**

(a) 100 m sprinter

> **Guided**

interval training ....

(b) Long distance runner

....

(c) Shot putter

....

(d) Games player

....

A 2 Two GCSE PE students were using fartlek training to improve their performance in their activities. One of the students played football; the other was a cross-country runner. Describe how each would adapt their use of this training method to follow the principle of specificity. **(4 marks)**

....

....

....

....

....

....

....

....

EXAM ALERT

Remember that specificity is about the sport, not the person.

Students have struggled with exam questions similar to this – **be prepared!** **ResultsPlus**

Principles of training: individual differences / rest and recovery

C

1   As part of an active, healthy lifestyle, an individual may apply the principles of training to produce a Personal Exercise Programme. Which of the following statements relates to the principle of individual needs in training?   **(1 mark)**

   ☐ **A**   Gradually making the body work harder because you are not as fit as someone else

   ☐ **B**   Following a standard recovery programme after injury

   ☐ **C**   Ensuring you have sufficient rest before continuing, even if this means following a different training programme than others in your team

   ☐ **D**   Tailoring your training to meet the demands of your sport, no one else's

F

2   While exercise is an important part of a healthy, active lifestyle, too much exercise can lead to injury. Name a principle of training, other than progressive overload, that can reduce the chance of injury.   **(1 mark)**

   ....

D

3   Explain the principle of individual differences and the value of applying it to your training programme.   **(3 marks)**

   ....

   ....

   ....

   ....

   ....

   ....

A

4   Apart from reducing the likelihood of sustaining injury through overuse, give another reason why the principle of rest and recovery is so important.   **(1 mark)**

   ....

   ....

Principles of training: FITT principle and reversibility

D

1 Applying the principles of training can help you to plan a balanced, healthy lifestyle, improve fitness and increase enjoyment during participation in physical activity.

Describe how a performer would use each aspect of the FITT principle to improve their fitness and level of performance when participating in physical activity. **(4 marks)**

Guided

FITT = frequency, intensity, time, type. The performer would use frequency by ....

....

....

....

....

....

....

....

B

2 The data in **Table 1** shows student resting heart rates over an eight-week period at the start of a weekly training session.

Note: All students had their heart rate recorded, even if they were unable to physically participate in the session that week.

Table 1

	Week							
Student	**1**	**2**	**3**	**4**	**5**	**6**	**7**	**8**
Student A	87	85	85	83	82	82	80	80
Student B	80	78	76	74	74	74	78	78
Student C	75	75	74	74	72	70	70	68

Explain which of the students has been affected by reversibility. **(2 marks)**

....

....

....

....

Value of goal setting and SMART targets

C

Guided

1 Give **three** reasons why the use of goal setting is considered to be good practice. **(3 marks)**

It helps you to plan your training by giving specific focus ....

....

....

....

....

....

C

2 SMART targets should be specific. Give an example of a specific target for a squash player who plays in the third team at their local leisure centre. **(1 mark)**

....

....

B

3 Give an example of a measurable target that the following performers may set themselves. **(5 marks)**

(a) A sprinter who currently runs 100 m in 14.10 seconds.

Guided

Decrease time to 14.0 seconds ....

....

Remember, for a target to be measurable you must be able to see if the target is met or not. It normally involves times or amounts.

(b) A high jumper who has a personal best of 1 m 50 cm.

....

(c) A games player who plays for the second team.

....

(d) A striker in the first team who scores five goals in the first six weeks of the season.

....

(e) A gymnast with a personal best tariff of 4.5.

....

SMART targets

B 1 For each of the following statements, explain why the target is not achievable for the performer described in the statement.

(a) A sprinter who currently runs 100 m in 14.10 seconds is set a target of 12.00 seconds within the next two weeks. **(2 marks)**

....

....

(b) A high jumper who has a personal best of third place when competing in county trials has been set a target of coming first at the next competition. **(2 marks)**

....

....

(c) A striker in the first team who scored five goals in the first six weeks of the season is set a target of scoring 20 in the next six weeks. **(2 marks)**

....

....

(d) A gymnast with a personal best tariff of 4.5 is set a target of achieving a 6.0 in their next competition. **(2 marks)**

....

....

C 2 Give an example of a time-bound SMART target for a squash player who plays in the third team at their local leisure centre. **(1 mark)**

....

....

Interval training

G 1 (a) Describe a characteristic of interval training. **(1 mark)**

....

....

B (b) Discuss whether it is suitable to use interval training for an endurance athlete. **(4 marks)**

Guided *Although normally used for anaerobic events,* ....

....

....

....

....

....

....

E (c) Give **two** examples of performers who may use a form of interval training as part of their training programme. **(2 marks)**

....

....

A (d) Explain how circuit training can be organised as an interval training session. **(3 marks)**

....

....

....

....

....

Continuous training

E 1 Identify **three** different types of activity where the performers would use continuous training to improve their fitness for their activity. **(3 marks)**

....

....

....

F 2 Which of the following is **not** an example of a continuous training method? **(1 mark)**

☐ **A** Continuous training

☐ **B** Circuit training

☐ **C** Weight training

☐ **D** Fartlek training

B

Guided 3 Explain how continuous training could be used to improve all aspects of health. **(4 marks)**

Any form of regular exercise can improve physical, social and mental aspects of health.

Continuous training would ....

....

....

....

....

E 4 Which **two** of the following would be considered to be a form of continuous training? **(2 marks)**

A Run for twenty minutes without a break

B Run for twenty minutes with a one minute break after the 5th; 10th and 15th minute

C Run for ten minutes then cycle for ten minutes without a break

D Run for one minute as fast as possible; rest for 1 minute; jog for 1 minute and repeat for twenty minutes

....

....

....

....

Fartlek training

1 (a) Describe why the area shown in Figure 1 below would be ideal for fartlek training.

(3 marks)

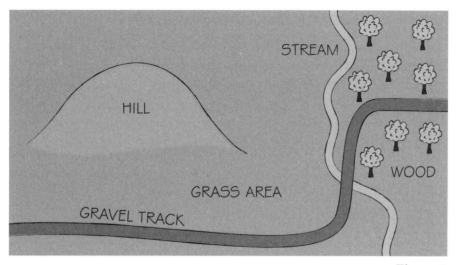

Figure 1

....

....

....

....

....

....

(b) Identify **two** different types of performers who would benefit from using this training.

(2 marks)

....

....

EXAM ALERT

Note the key word **different**. A footballer would be a good example, but not if your other example is a rugby player, as they would both be the same types of player (games players).

Students have struggled with exam questions similar to this – **be prepared!**   ResultsPlus

(c) Identify **two** components of fitness that would be most likely to improve as a result of using this training.

(2 marks)

....

....

....

....

Circuit training

C

1 **(a)** Use the box below to draw a plan for a six-station circuit training session for someone who wanted to improve a variety of health-related and skill-related aspects of fitness.

You must include stations to develop at least **two** different components of health-related exercise and **two** different components of skill-related fitness in your circuit.

(6 marks)

> Read **all** parts of the question first, as your choice of stations in part (a) will impact on your answers to the following parts of the question.

C

(b) For each station, state the component of fitness it will improve.   **(6 marks)**

	Component of fitness improved
Station 1	
Station 2	
Station 3	
Station 4	
Station 5	
Station 6	

D

> Guided

(c) Explain why you have placed the stations in the order you have.   **(2 marks)**

It is a good idea to alternate muscle groups being worked because ....

....

Weight training

C 1 John was hoping to improve his fitness and his friends recommended he should try weight training.

(a) Describe weight training as a method of training, giving **two** examples of typical exercises that might be included in a programme. **(4 marks)**

....

....

....

....

....

....

....

F (b) Which components of fitness does weight training help to develop? **(2 marks)**

....

....

....

....

B (c) Describe how a weight training programme could be adapted for different performers of different levels of physical fitness. **(3 marks)**

....

....

....

....

....

....

C (d) State how a weight training session would differ for an endurance athlete compared to a power athlete. **(1 mark)**

....

....

Cross training

D 1 (a) Describe the training method 'cross training'. **(2 marks)**

....

....

....

....

C (b) Using an example, explain why someone might use cross training as a way of keeping fit. **(2 marks)**

....

....

....

....

B (c) Describe **four** advantages of cross training as a method of training. **(8 marks)**

....

....

....

....

....

....

....

....

....

....

....

Remember that this is a revision question and you would not have an 8 mark question in your exam. Whatever the question total, remember to use the number of marks available as a guide. To answer this question well, give **four** advantages of cross training with an **explanation** of how each **advantage** is achieved.

Exercise session: warm-up

B 1 (a) Warm ups should be conducted before taking part in any form of physical activity.

Complete the table below.

- Name, in the correct order, the **three** phases of a warm up. **(3 marks)**
- Give an example of a typical activity associated with that phase of the warm up.

(3 marks)

Phase of warm up	Example activity associated with phase of warm up

B (b) Using examples, explain why the final phase of the warm up would vary, depending on the activity the performer was about to take part in. **(3 marks)**

....

....

....

....

....

....

D (c) Give **two** physical reasons why players should warm up before playing sport. **(2 marks)**

....

....

....

....

EXAM ALERT

The advice is usually to give different examples or reasons, but this question is asking specifically for **two** physical reasons. Make sure you read the question carefully and highlight the key words in the question.

Students have struggled with exam questions similar to this – **be prepared!** ResultsPlus

Exercise session: main session and cool-down

1 Luke is being assessed as a leader in one of his GCSE PE practical activities.

C

   (a) After running the main session, what should Luke ensure he does before the end of the training session with his group? **(1 mark)**

....

D

   (b) Using suitable examples, describe the phases of this part of the training session.

                                                             (4 marks)

....

....

....

....

....

....

G

   (c) What will happen to the intensity of exercise during this final stage of the training session? **(1 mark)**

....

C

Guided

   (d) Give **four** reasons why it is important that Luke carries out these activities at the end of his training session. **(4 marks)**

    To slowly return the body to its resting state and ....

....

....

....

....

....

EXAM ALERT

Always read the question and make sure that you give the number of reasons you've been asked for in the question.	Students have struggled with exam questions similar to this – **be prepared!** ResultsPlus

Exercise session: endurance

A

1 (a) Identify **three** different training methods that could be adapted to improve a performer's cardiovascular fitness and muscular endurance.   **(3 marks)**

....

....

....

A

(b) Describe how **two** of the training methods you identified in (a) could be used to improve cardiovascular fitness and muscular endurance for a named activity.

Activity: ....

• Training method 1:   **(3 marks)**

Guided

Circuit training. The stations to be included would be those that allowed the performer to

work aerobically ....

....

....

....

....

....

• Training method 2:   **(3 marks)**

....

....

....

....

....

....

> Think carefully about your choice of training method. The question is asking how to improve cardiovascular fitness and muscular endurance, therefore you will need training methods that use aerobic work rather than anaerobic.

Exercise session: power

A   1   (a)   Identify **three** different training methods that could be adapted for use by a performer who needs high levels of power for their activity.   **(3 marks)**

....

....

....

A   (b)   Describe how **two** of the training methods you identified in (a) could be used to improve power.

   •   Training method 1:   **(3 marks)**

> **Guided**

Circuit training. The stations to be included would be those that allowed the performer

to work anaerobically ....

....

....

....

....

   •   Training method 2:   **(3 marks)**

....

....

....

....

....

D   (c)   Identify **two** principles of training that a performer should apply to ensure power is developed in their training sessions.   **(2 marks)**

....

....

Heart rates and graphs

Martin is a keen sportsman and wants to get fitter. During training, Martin measures his heart rate at various points during his exercise sessions.

C

1 **(a)** What information can Martin gain by recording his resting heart rate over a period of several weeks before each of his exercise sessions?   **(3 marks)**

....

....

....

....

(b) The graph below shows Martin's heart rate at rest, during exercise and immediately after the first part of the training session finishes.

> Make sure you understand what is meant by resting heart rate, working heart rate and recovery rate and be able to evaluate results on a graph.

F

(i) How many minutes into the session did Martin begin to exercise? Give a reason for your answer.   **(2 marks)**

....

....

....

C

(ii) Using the graph, explain what you think happened to Martin's workload between the 9th and the 10th minute.   **(2 marks)**

....

....

D

(iii) Explain whether Martin has fully recovered from exercise after 13 minutes.

(2 marks)

....

....

....

> Use the information on the graph to help you

EXAM ALERT

> Students in the past have struggled to read and plot graphs – make sure you're confident that you can do this.

> Students have struggled with exam questions similar to this – **be prepared!**   ResultsPlus

Setting training target zones

C 1 Explain the terms 'target zone' and 'training thresholds', and how they should be used.

(3 marks)

....

....

....

....

....

B 2 **(a)** Riana is helping her younger sister who is 16 with her fitness programme, as she realises the importance of exercise to maintain a healthy, active lifestyle.

How would Riana calculate her sister's target zone to improve her aerobic fitness?

(3 marks)

220 – ....

....

....

....

....

A **(b)** Jed is a long distance runner and Mike is a sprinter. Explain why they would use different heart rate target zones within their training.   **(3 marks)**

....

....

....

....

....

....

Requirements of a balanced diet

1   In order to maintain a high level of performance, athletes need a good balance between exercise, diet, work and rest.

Figure 1 shows some suggested proportions for the different components that make up a balanced diet.

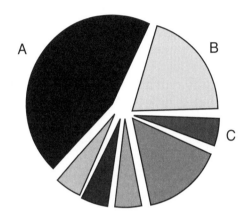

Figure 1 Suggested proportions of a balanced diet

D

Guided

(i)   List the **seven** components that should be included within a balanced diet.   **(1 mark)**

Carbohydrates ....

....

....

....

....

....

....

> Not all seven components are 'food groups'.

C

(ii)   Identify the **three** macronutrients labelled as A, B and C in **Figure 1**.   **(3 marks)**

A represents ....

B represents ....

C represents ....

EXAM ALERT

The sizes of the 'slices' A, B and C will vary from graph to graph, so in this case A is the component you should eat most of in your diet.

Students have struggled with exam questions similar to this – **be prepared!**   ResultsPlus

Macronutrients

E

1 Protein is a macronutrient and is an essential part of the diet. Which of the following statements correctly describes why protein is an essential part of the diet? **(1 mark)**

☐ **A** To help digestion

☐ **B** To transport oxygen during activity

☐ **C** To increase blood flow during exercise

☐ **D** To help with muscle growth as a result of training adaptations

C

2 Give **two** reasons why different athletes will eat different quantities of macronutrients.

(2 marks)

....

....

....

....

EXAM ALERT

Remember that you can make notes to help clarify the requirements of a question. This is a challenging question, so work out exactly what is being asked for before you attempt an answer.

Students have struggled with exam questions similar to this – **be prepared!** ResultsPlus

B

3 Fats are macronutrients that provide the body with energy. Explain the importance of **two** other macronutrients in maintaining an active lifestyle. **(4 marks)**

....

....

....

Note the reference to an active lifestyle. How do these macronutrients help keep us active?

....

....

....

....

....

Micronutrients

1 Micronutrients are required for a balanced diet.

Ⓐ

(a) Describe what is meant by the term 'micronutrient'. **(4 marks)**

....

....

....

....

(b) Complete the table below.

Ⓔ

Ⓒ

(i) Name **two** different types of micronutrient. **(2 marks)**

(ii) Give **two** examples of each type of micronutrient. **(4 marks)**

> **Guided**

Types of micronutrient		Examples of each type of micronutrient	
1		1	Vitamin C
		2	
2		1	
		2	

Ⓐ

(c) For each of your examples in (b) above, explain how they help to maintain a healthy lifestyle. **(4 marks)**

....

....

....

....

....

....

....

....

Timing of dietary intake

1 Use the images below to help you explain why you should consider the timing of your dietary intake.

(5 marks)

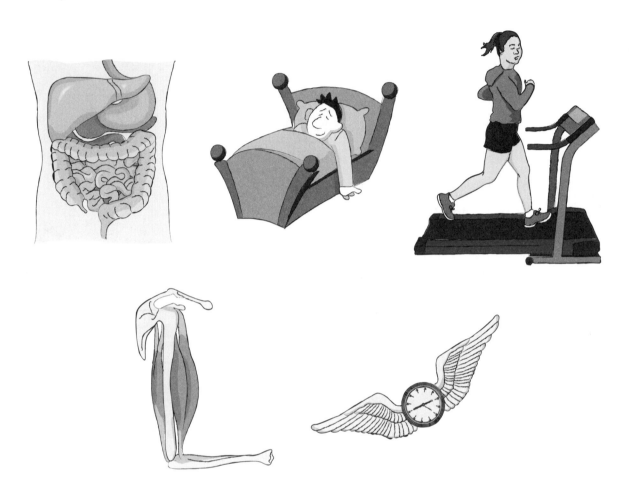

....

....

....

....

....

....

....

....

....

EXAM ALERT

Some questions contain images. They are there to support you, so make sure you use them to guide your answer.

Students have struggled with this topic in recent exams – **be prepared!**

ResultsPlus

Redistribution of blood flow

B

Guided

1 (a) Using examples, describe what is meant by the term 'blood shunting'. **(3 marks)**

Blood shunting is the term for the process when blood flow to different parts of the

body is altered. For example, when exercising ....

....

....

....

(b) As demands on the body increase due to exercise, blood flow to different parts of the body alters.

Explain how and why blood flow to the digestive system is altered during exercise.

(4 marks)

....

....

....

....

....

....

....

....

(c) Why is this beneficial for the performer, provided they haven't recently eaten? **(2 marks)**

....

....

....

....

Mesomorphs

G 1 The performers in each of the images on this page have the same extreme body type. Name the body type. **(1 mark)**

....

B 2 **(a)** Using examples from the images, identify **four** characteristics of this extreme body type. **(4 marks)**

....

....

....

....

....

(b) Using examples, explain how **two** of the characteristics you have identified in (a) are an advantage to the performers in the images. **(4 marks)**

....

....

....

....

....

C 3 Extreme mesomorph body types are suited to specific sporting activities.

Identify **three** common components of health-related exercise or skill-related fitness demands of activities where an extreme mesomorph body type would be an advantage. **(3 marks)**

Strength ....

> Guided

....

....

Ectomorphs and endomorphs

C 1 The performer in Figure 1 has some characteristics of an endomorph body type.

Figure 1

    (a) Identify **three** characteristics of this extreme body type.   **(3 marks)**

....

....

....

....

....

    (b) Explain how **one** of the characteristics you have identified in (a) could be an advantage in the shot putt.   **(2 marks)**

....

....

....

....

G 2 Using examples, explain how **two** of the characteristics of an extreme ectomorph body type would be an advantage to the performer in Figure 2.   **(4 marks)**

> **Guided**

Long frame so tall, this means centre of gravity is higher. This is an advantage in the high jump because

Figure 2

....

....

....

....

F 3 Tick **three** options from the following nine activities where an ectomorph body type would be an advantage.   **(3 marks)**

☐ Football goalkeeper   ☐ Jockey   ☐ Horse rider

☐ Basketball player   ☐ Netball Goal Shooter   ☐ Long jumper

☐ Gymnast   ☐ Wrestler   ☐ Golfer

Factors affecting optimum weight

(D) 1 Explain the term 'optimum weight'. **(2 marks)**

....

....

(B) 2 Outline how **four** different factors could cause a variation in an individual's
optimum weight. **(8 marks)**

Guided Your height will affect your optimum weight, the taller you are the more you will weigh ....

....

....

....

....

....

....

....

(D) 3 Use examples to demonstrate why and how optimum weight can be different in one
activity compared with another. **(4 marks)**

Guided A jockey's optimum weight will be different from a ....

....

....

....

....

....

....

Anorexia and underweight

D   1   Explain the term 'anorexia'. **(2 marks)**

....

....

A   2   Explain how the following symptoms of anorexia would impact on achieving sustained involvement in physical activity.

- Eats very little, if at all, or restrict certain foods, such as those containing fat
- Is obsessed with exercise
- Is very tired
- Is dehydrated **(4 marks)**

....

....

....

....

....

....

....

....

D   3   Explain the difference between anorexia and underweight. **(2 marks)**

....

....

....

....

Overweight, overfat, obese

1   Being **overweight**, **overfat** and **obese** are all conditions that can have a negative impact on the health of an individual.

G

(a) Write each of these terms in one of the boxes below, placing the most dangerous condition in the first box, and the least dangerous to health in the third box.   **(2 marks)**

Most dangerous ⟶ Least dangerous

B

(b) Explain why you have placed the terms in the order you chose.   **(3 marks)**

....

....

....

....

....

....

....

....

D

2   How could sustained involvement in physical activity protect against obesity?   **(2 marks)**

....

....

....

....

Anabolic steroids

B 1 Anabolic steroids can cause liver damage and premature heart disease. Identify **three** other possible health risks from taking anabolic steroids. **(3 marks)**

....

....

....

A 2 Explain why a sprinter may be more tempted to take anabolic steroids than a long distance runner. **(3 marks)**

....

....

....

....

....

....

EXAM ALERT

The command word is 'explain', so for a 3 mark question, your answer must be in more depth than for a one-mark question.

Students have struggled with exam questions similar to this – **be prepared!** ResultsPlus

C 3 Explain why anabolic steroid use is thought to be equivalent to cheating. **(3 marks)**

....

....

....

....

....

....

Beta blockers

B

1   Beta blockers can be prescribed by doctors to help patients relax. Discuss **why** this might be helpful to **some** sports performers but not others.   **(6 marks)**

> The word 'some' is emphasised in the question. Try to think why some performers might take beta blockers, yet others wouldn't.

....

....

....

....

....

....

....

....

C

2   Performance enhancing drugs have harmful side-effects.

Identify **two** harmful side-effects that a performer could experience if they took beta blockers.   **(2 marks)**

....

....

....

....

D

3   The use of beta blockers by elite performers is banned.

Explain why some performers will still risk taking beta blockers.   **(3 marks)**

....

....

....

E

4   Identify **two** activities where performers could gain an advantage if they took beta blockers
   (2 marks)

....

....

....

Diuretics

C 1 One possible side-effect of taking diuretics is dehydration.

(a) Outline why dehydration can occur if a performer takes diuretics.   **(2 marks)**

....

....

....

....

(b) Identify **two** other side-effects from taking diuretics and explain why they are disadvantages for the performer.   **(4 marks)**

....

....

....

....

....

....

....

(c) Identify **two** activities where performers might take a diuretic before their performance and explain why taking the diuretic gives them an advantage.   **(3 marks)**

> **Guided**

Horse racing – a jockey may take a diuretic to help by

> Think about two different reasons why people take this category of drug – this should help you choose the different activities.

....

....

....

....

....

EXAM ALERT

Don't just state the activities. Think about the benefits of diuretics and then think who would gain from these benefits.

Students have struggled with exam questions similar to this – **be prepared!**   ResultsPlus

Narcotic analgesics

C 1 This is a list of possible harmful side effects from taking performance-enhancing drugs is listed below.

(a) Tick **two** that relate to narcotic analgesics. **(2 marks)**

☐ Vomiting

☐ Insomnia

☐ Acne

☐ Slow heart rate

☐ Facial hair in women

☐ Loss of concentration

☐ Heart failure

☐ Kidney damage

☐ Tiredness

(b) State **one** way in which one of the side effects you selected in (a) could be potentially harmful to health. **(1 mark)**

....

....

E 2 (a) Explain why a performer in an event of your choice might take narcotic analgesics. **(2 marks)**

▷ **Guided** ▷

A tennis player may take narcotic analgesics after they ....

....

....

....

D (b) Explain why narcotic analgesics are banned. **(2 marks)**

....

....

....

....

EXAM ALERT

Think about your answer. You are not specifically asked why performers are tempted to take these drugs – but if you know the reason for that, it will help you think about why they are banned.

Students have struggled with exam questions similar to this – **be prepared!**   ResultsPlus

Stimulants

Caffeine is a stimulant that is readily available to all. In large doses it becomes an illegal performance-enhancing drug.

(A) 1 **(a)** Explain **two** health risks associated with taking stimulants. **(4 marks)**

....

....

....

....

....

....

....

(B) **(b)** Explain **two** non-health risks to the performer of taking stimulants. **(4 marks)**

....

....

....

....

....

....

....

....

(B) 2 Performers who test positive for stimulants will be disqualified from competition. Despite this risk, explain why boxers might be tempted to take them. **(3 marks)**

....

....

....

....

....

Peptide hormones

A 1 Erythropoietin (EPO) is an example of a peptide hormone. Explain why a long-distance runner would be **more** tempted to take EPO than a sprinter. **(4 marks)**

....

....

....

....

....

....

....

....

C 2 This is a list of possible harmful side-effects from taking performance-enhancing drugs. Tick **two** that relate to the peptide hormone erythropoietin (EPO). **(2 marks)**

> Don't tick more answers than you are asked for in the question. If you do, it is likely that none of your answers will count.

☐ Dehydration

☐ Insomnia

☐ Acne

☐ Slow heart rate

☐ Facial hair in women

☐ Loss of concentration

☐ Heart failure

☐ Increased viscosity of the blood

☐ Tiredness

☐ Masks injury

☐ Nausea and vomiting

Recreational drugs

D

1 (a) Identify **two** body systems that are negatively impacted by smoking. **(2 marks)**

....

....

(b) Smoking and drinking alcohol are considered to be socially acceptable or recreational forms of drug taking.

(i) How does this differ from taking performance-enhancing drugs? **(1 mark)**

....

....

(ii) There are known health risks associated with smoking and drinking alcohol. Why are athletes still allowed to take these types of drugs? **(1 mark)**

....

....

(c) Identify and explain a health risk associated with smoking. **(2 marks)**

....

....

....

....

(d) Identify and explain a health risk associated with drinking alcohol. **(2 marks)**

....

....

....

....

Reducing risk through personal readiness

1 Bruno is an all-round sports performer. He participates in many different sporting activities and is aware of a number of risks associated with his activities.

D

> **Guided**

(a) Complete the table for each named activity:

- Identify a typical risk associated with that activity.

- Outline how the risk may occur.

Each risk should be different. **(8 marks)**

Activity	Typical risk	How risk may occur
Judo	Bruising	By being thrown to the floor by opponent
Football		
High diving (swimming)		
Boxing		

C

(b) Explain how Bruno should reduce the risk you have identified in the table above for football. **(3 marks)**

....

....

....

....

....

....

G

2 Identify the risks that could be reduced through the use of the following risk reduction methods. **(3 marks)**

(a) Warm up

....

(b) Mouth guard

....

(c) Checking for debris such as glass on a pitch before play

....

Reducing risk through other measures

D   1   Complete the following table by:

- Identifying a risk reduction measure relevant to the activity in the image.   **(4 marks)**

- Stating how the identified risk reduction measure reduces risk associated with the activity.   **(4 marks)**

Use a **different** risk reduction measure for each answer.

Activity where used	Risk reduction measure relevant to the image	How risk is reduced through this measure

EXAM ALERT

Note the instruction in the question to give a different example for each. If you use the same example twice, you will not be credited.

Students have struggled with exam questions similar to this – **be prepared!**   ResultsPlus

Cardiovascular system and exercise

B   1 **(a)** Explain this equation:

Cardiac output = HR × SV   **(3 marks)**

....

....

....

C   **(b)** What happens to cardiac output during exercise and how is this achieved?   **(3 marks)**

....

....

....

C   **(c)** Exercise causes an increase in demand on the cardiovascular system.

Explain **one** benefit of these immediate changes to a performer.   **(3 marks)**

....

....

....

....

....

D   2 Which of the following is **not** an immediate effect of exercise on the cardiovascular system?

(1 mark)

☐ **A** Increase in heart rate

☐ **B** Increase in stroke volume

☐ **C** Increase in breathing rate

☐ **D** Increase in systolic blood pressure

Cardiovascular system: adaptations 1

1 The hearts in the image are graphical representations of the heart of a trained athlete and the heart of a non-trained individual.

Heart A   Heart B

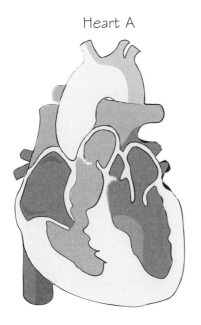   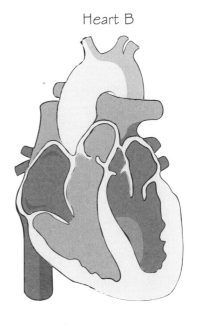

D **(a)** Which heart, A or B, is representative of the trained athlete?   **(1 mark)**

....

B **(b)** Explain your answer to (a).   **(3 marks)**

....

....

....

....

C 2 Identify and explain **two** long-term benefits of regular training on the cardiovascular system.
        (4 marks)

Guided   Increased strength of heart therefore ....

....

....

....

....

Had a go ☐ Nearly there ☐ Nailed it! ☐

Cardiovascular system: adaptations 2

D 1 One training adaptation that occurs as a result of regular participation in physical activity is that the heart rate returns to resting heart rate more quickly than before. Explain why this is an advantage when participating in physical activity. **(1 mark)**

....

....

B 2 One long-term adaptation of regular participation in physical activity is capillarisation. Explain the benefit of an increase in capillarisation to a hockey player. **(3 marks)**

....

....

....

....

....

....

A 3 **(a)** What impact does regular training have on the equation below, when the performer is resting? **(1 mark)**

Cardiac output = HR × SV

....

(b) Explain your answer to (a). **(2 marks)**

....

....

....

F 4 Which of the following resting heart rate values is the most likely for a trained athlete? **(1 mark)**

☐ **A** 65 bpm

☐ **B** 65 mpg

☐ **C** 90 bpm

☐ **D** 220 bpm

Blood pressure and cholesterol

C 1 Name the **two** different types of blood pressure. **(2 marks)**

....

....

B 2 Why are there two different types of blood pressure, rather than just one? **(3 marks)**

....

....

....

B 3 Explain why blood pressure increases as a result of exercise. **(3 marks)**

....

....

....

> Students often find this topic difficult. Remember to use the number of marks available as a guide to the number of statements you make.

C 4 Which of the two types of blood pressure is higher in a healthy adult, and why? **(3 marks)**

....

....

....

C 5 Which of the following can cause deposits to build up in the arteries, making it harder for blood to circulate? **(1 mark)**

☐ **A** Light density lipoprotein

☐ **B** Low density lipoprotein

☐ **C** High density lipoprotein

☐ **D** Medium density lipoprotein

Respiratory system and exercise

G 1 (a) Identify an immediate effect of exercise on breathing rate. **(1 mark)**

....

D (b) Explain how the immediate effect you identified in (a) helps the performer. **(3 marks)**

....

....

....

....

G (c) Which of the following is an immediate effect of exercise and physical activity on the respiratory system? **(1 mark)**

☐ **A** Increased depth of breathing

☐ **B** Increased heart rate

☐ **C** Increased lung capacity

☐ **D** Increased stroke volume

B 2 Complete the sentence below by filling in the spaces to describe a consequence of anaerobic exercise. **(5 marks)**

.... debt is the amount of .... required

.... anaerobic exercise .... that

normally used at ....

B 3 Apart from the health risks, explain how smoking might affect performance in physical activity, giving an example. **(3 marks)**

....

....

....

....

....

....

Respiratory system: adaptations

1 One adaptation of regular exercise on the respiratory system is an increase in the number of alveoli in the lungs.

(D) **(a)** Identify **two** other long-term effects of regular participation on the respiratory system.

(2 marks)

....

....

(D) **(b) (i)** Give an example of a performer who would benefit from an increase in the number of alveoli in the lungs. **(1 mark)**

....

(B) **(ii)** Explain why an increase in the number of alveoli used would be a benefit to the performer you identified in (b) (i). **(3 marks)**

....

....

....

....

(D) **(c) (i)** Give an example of a performer where an increase in the number of alveoli used in the lungs would have little or no impact on performance. **(1 mark)**

....

(C) **(ii)** Explain why an increase in the number of alveoli used would have little or no impact on the performer you identified in (c) (i). **(2 marks)**

....

....

....

(C) **2** What is meant by the term 'vital capacity'? **(1 mark)**

....

....

Had a go ☐ Nearly there ☐ Nailed it! ☐

Antagonistic muscle pairs: biceps and triceps

G

1 Name the muscle, at the front of the upper arm, identified as A in **Figure 1**. **(1 mark)**

....

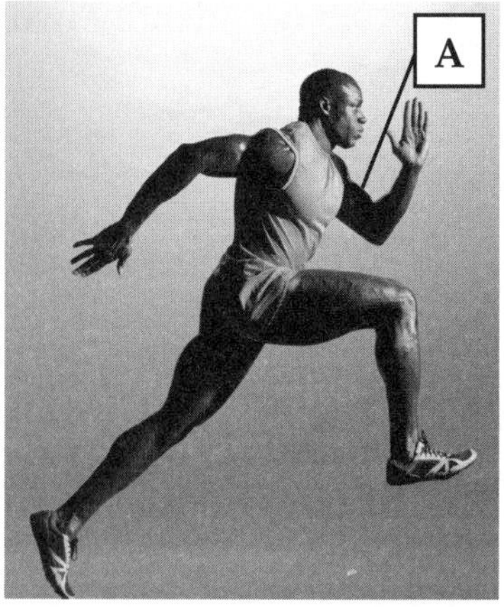

Figure 1

E

2 (a) Explain the term **antagonistic muscle pairs**. **(2 marks)**

....

....

....

....

G

(b) Name the muscle that works antagonistically with muscle A in **Figure 1**. **(1 mark)**

....

D

(c) Explain how these muscles act as an antagonistic pair. **(2 marks)**

....

....

....

....

E

(d) How does the ability to use his arm muscles as an antagonistic pair help the sprinter in his performance? **(1 mark)**

....

C

(e) Identify the range of movement at the elbow that results from the sprinter's arm muscles working antagonistically. **(1 mark)**

....

....

Remember to specifically relate your answer to sprinting.

Students have struggled with exam questions similar to this – **be prepared!** ResultsPlus

Antagonistic muscle pairs: quadriceps and hamstrings

E

1 (a) (i) Name the muscle at the front of the thigh, identified as B in **Figure 1**. **(1 mark)**

....

C

(ii) Identify the role of muscle B. **(1 mark)**

....

....

Figure 1

B

(b) Give examples from **three** different sporting activities of how this muscle is used. **(3 marks)**

> **Guided**

One example is the follow through with the leg after taking a shot at goal in football

....

....

....

....

> Note the word 'different' in the question: make sure all three examples are from different sports.

> Students have struggled with exam questions similar to this – **be prepared!** ResultsPlus

E

(c) (i) Name the muscle that works antagonistically with muscle A in **Figure 1**. **(1 mark)**

....

C

(ii) Identify the role of this antagonistic muscle. **(1 mark)**

....

....

B

(iii) Give an example of the use of this muscle, when acting as an agonist, in physical activity. **(1 mark)**

....

....

Gluteals, gastrocnemius and deltoid

F   1   Choose the appropriate word from the box to complete the following statements about muscles and their role during physical activity. **(4 marks)**

Abducting   hip   flexing   shoulder   leg   buttocks   arm   extending   calf   vertebrae

The gluteals are located in the .... They are responsible

for .... the leg at the hip. The deltoid muscle is found

in the .... and is responsible for movement of the

upper ....

B   2   Name the muscle that acts as the agonist in each of the following movements.

    (a)   The overarm bowling action in cricket   **(1 mark)**

    ....

    (b)   Pointing the toes when performing a trampolining routine   **(1 mark)**

    ....

B   3   Give **two** different examples of the use of the deltoids in physical activity.

    Your answers must be different to any other sporting examples on this page.   **(2 marks)**

    ....

    ....

    ....

    ....

C   4   Identify the role of the gluteals in this image.   **(1 mark)**

    ....

    ....

Trapezius, latissimus dorsi, pectorals and abdominals

F

1 (a) (i) Using the image of the squash player below, label the location of the pectorals and the abdominals. **(2 marks)**

A

(ii) Give an example of how the squash player will use each of these muscles during a game. **(2 marks)**

....

....

....

....

C

2 Identify the muscles labelled A and B in the image below and explain their role.

Muscle A is the ....

(1 mark)

Muscle B is the ....

(1 mark)

The role of muscle A is

....

....

The role of muscle B is ....

....

(2 marks)

The muscular system and exercise

D   1   What is meant by the terms **isotonic** and **isometric** muscle contraction?   **(2 marks)**

....

....

....

....

F   2   Identify whether the actions shown in the images below are examples of isometric or
isotonic muscle contractions.   **(4 marks)**

| Arm wrestle when equal force is applied by each competitor. | Moment of stillness just prior to pushing off to dive. | Running in a long-distance race. | Both teams applying equal force in a tug-of-war so the rope is still. |

....

C   3   As soon as we begin to exercise, our body systems work harder to cope with the additional
demands being made upon them.

Identify **three** immediate effects of exercise on our muscular system.   **(3 marks)**

....

....

....

....

EXAM ALERT

Make sure you know the difference between immediate and long-term effects of exercise.

Students have struggled with exam questions similar to this – **be prepared!**

ResultsPlus

B   4   Using **one** of your answers to question 3, explain why the muscular system responds in this
way to exercise.   **(2 marks)**

....

....

....

The muscular system: adaptations

G 1 Which of the following statements is **not** a long-term effect of regular physical activity on the muscular system? **(1 mark)**

☐ **A** Increased strength of muscles

☐ **B** Increased muscular hypertrophy

☐ **C** Increased muscular atrophy

☐ **D** Increased myoglobin stores

B 2 The body adapts as a result of regular training, providing long-term benefits for those that train. For the named activity explain **two** adaptations to the muscular system which would benefit performance. **(4 marks)**

Named activity:

> **Guided**

A .... would benefit due to increased size and ....

....

....

....

....

....

B 3 State the long-term training effect on the muscular system that results in more oxygen being available for uptake by the muscles. **(1 mark)**

....

D 4 What does the term **muscular hypertrophy** mean? **(1 mark)**

....

G 5 Which of the following statements is **not** a long-term effect of regular physical activity on the muscular system? **(1 mark)**

☐ **A** Increased strength

☐ **B** Increased power

☐ **C** Increased cardiovascular fitness

☐ **D** Increased muscular endurance

Functions of the skeletal system

D 1 The skeleton has many functions.

(a) One of the functions of the skeleton is to provide protection. Give **two** examples from physical activity to explain how the skeleton provides protection. **(4 marks)**

> **Guided**

The skull protects the brain if hit in the head by a hockey stick ....

..The.. ....

....

....

(b) In the table below, state **two** functions of the skeleton other than protection, and give an example of their use in physical activity. **(4 marks)**

Function of the skeleton	Example of use in physical activity

C 2 For each image, identify a **different** role of the skeletal system and describe how the role is achieved in the image **(4 marks)**

Figure 1 ....

....

....

....

Figure 1

Figure 2 ....

....

....

....

Figure 2

E 3 Choose words from the box to complete the statement below. **(4 marks)**

| muscles ligaments bones movement levers support |

.... act as .... to provide

.... when contracting ....

(connected via a tendon) pulls them.

What you need to know about joints

G   **1**   Define the term 'joint'.

(a) ....

(1 mark)

(b) For each of the images, A, B, C and D:

- name the joint indicated by the arrow
- state the **type** of joint indicated by the arrow.

(8 marks)

Joint A

Name ....

Type ....

A

Joint B

Name ....

Type ....

B

Joint C

Name ....

Type ....

C

Joint D

Name ....

Type ....

D

Had a go ☐ Nearly there ☐ Nailed it! ☐

Range of movement at joints 1

  1 (a) Describe the term 'flexion' in relation to movement at a joint, and give an example from physical activity. **(2 marks)**

....

....

(b) Describe the term 'extension' in relation to movement at a joint, and give an example from physical activity. **(2 marks)**

....

....

  EXAM ALERT

Make sure that any example you give is very clearly an example of the specific movement asked for. Kicking a football would be too vague.

Students have struggled with exam questions similar to this – **be prepared!** ResultsPlus

  2 The following images show people participating in a range of physical activities.

(a) Circle all occasions in **Figure 1** and **Figure 2** where flexion is occurring and name the joint.

Guided

.......Hip.......

Figure 1 (2 marks)

Figure 2 (3 marks)

(b) Circle all occasions in **Figure 3** and **Figure 4** where extension is occurring and name the joint.

Figure 3 (3 marks)

Figure 4 (1 mark)

Range of movement at joints 2

F   1   **(a)** Describe the term **abduction** in relation to movement at a joint and give an example from physical activity.   **(2 marks)**

....

....

   (b) Describe the term **rotation** in relation to movement at a joint and give an example from physical activity.   **(2 marks)**

....

....

D   2   The following images show people participating in physical activities.

   (a) Which of **Figure 1** or **Figure 2** shows abduction at the shoulder?   **(1 mark)**

Figure 1   Figure 2

....

   (b) Which of the following is correct in identifying movement at the joints in **Figure 3** and **Figure 4**?   **(1 mark)**

     ☐   **A**   There is no rotation taking place in either image

     ☐   **B**   Abduction at the knee can be seen in Figure 4

     ☐   **C**   Both images show abduction of the arm at the shoulder

     ☐   **D**   The swimmer in Figure 3 is rotating the arm at the elbow

Figure 3   Figure 4

The skeletal system and exercise

E 1 (a) (i) Which **one** of the following activities is **most** likely to reduce the chance of osteoporosis? **(1 mark)**

Walking

Cycling

Rowing

Bobsleigh

....

D (ii) Name **two** other weight-bearing activities. **(2 marks)**

....

....

D (b) State the difference between weight-bearing activities and non-weight bearing activities. **(1 mark)**

....

....

B (c) Give **four** advantages of weight-bearing activities for the skeletal system. **(4 marks)**

....

....

....

....

G 2 Which of the following mineral is associated with stronger bones? **(1 mark)**

☐ **A** Calcium   ☐ **C** Sodium

☐ **B** Iron   ☐ **D** Granite

B 3 Give a reason why it is beneficial to have stronger bones when taking part in physical activity. **(1 mark)**

....

Potential injuries: fractures

F 1 (a) What type of injury is shown in images A, B, C and D below? **(1 mark)**

....

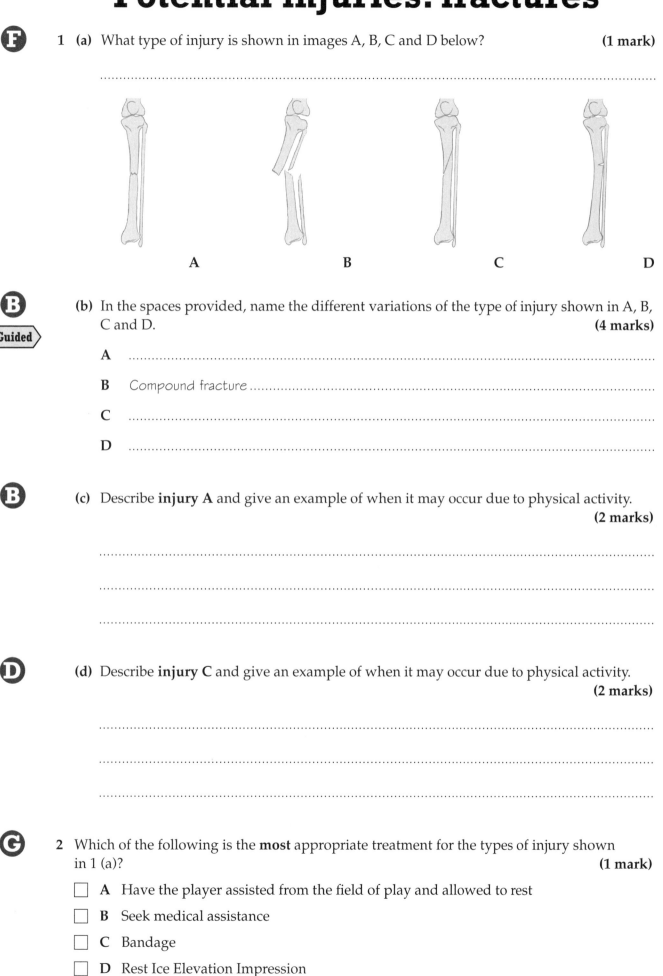

| A | B | C | D |

B

Guided

(b) In the spaces provided, name the different variations of the type of injury shown in A, B, C and D. **(4 marks)**

A ....

B   Compound fracture ....

C ....

D ....

B (c) Describe **injury A** and give an example of when it may occur due to physical activity.
(2 marks)

....

....

....

D (d) Describe **injury C** and give an example of when it may occur due to physical activity.
(2 marks)

....

....

....

G 2 Which of the following is the **most** appropriate treatment for the types of injury shown in 1 (a)? **(1 mark)**

☐ **A** Have the player assisted from the field of play and allowed to rest

☐ **B** Seek medical assistance

☐ **C** Bandage

☐ **D** Rest Ice Elevation Impression

Potential injuries: joint injuries

C 1 Which of the following is the correct description of golfer's elbow? **(1 mark)**

☐ **A** Golfer's elbow is a joint injury where the pain is felt on the inside of the elbow

☐ **B** Golfer's elbow is a joint injury where the pain is felt on the outside of the elbow

☐ **C** Golfer's elbow is where a joint comes out of place

☐ **D** Golfer's elbow is where the bone bends on one side and breaks on the other

D 2 Identify **one** potential cause of golfer's elbow. **(1 mark)**

....

....

E 3 Describe what happens if a joint becomes dislocated. **(2 marks)**

....

....

....

....

C 4 Give an example from physical activity of when a joint may become dislocated. **(1 mark)**

....

....

D 5 What type of injury is a dislocation? **(1 mark)**

☐ **A** Fracture

☐ **B** Deep bruising

☐ **C** Joint injury

☐ **D** Sprain

B 6 What causes the pain associated with injuries, such as tennis elbow and golfer's elbow?

(1 mark)

....

....

Potential injuries: sprains and torn cartilage

B   1   Complete the table below.

- Chose **two** common joint injuries from the box.
- Give a brief description of the injury.
- Give a common symptom of that injury.   **(4 marks)**

torn cartilage   graze   sprain   bruising   strain   cut

	Injury	Description	Symptom
(a)			
(b)			

EXAM ALERT

In questions like this, start by looking for the key term – joint injuries – then discount any injuries that are not joint injuries.

Students have struggled with exam questions similar to this – **be prepared!**   ResultsPlus

F   2   **(a)**   Which of the following is a common treatment for joint injuries?   **(1 mark)**

☐ **A**   D.R.A.B.C.

☐ **B**   R.I.C.E.

☐ **C**   S.P.O.R.T.

☐ **D**   R.Y.C.E.

Make sure you know the acronym **and** what the letters represent.

E   **(b)**   For your choice of answer to (a), state the word that each initial letter represents.

(4 marks)

....

....

....

....

....

Exam skills: multiple choice questions

For each question, choose an answer, A, B, C or D, and put a cross in the box ☒.

If you change your mind about an answer, put a line through the box ☒ and then mark your new answer with a cross ☒.

(F) 1 Which of the following is not a macronutrient? **(1 mark)**

☐ **A** Vitamins   ☐ **C** Fats

☐ **B** Carbohydrates   ☐ **D** Proteins

(D) 2 Which of the following is not a long-term effect of physical activity on the respiratory system? **(1 mark)**

☐ **A** Increased number of alveoli   ☐ **C** Increased strength of the diaphragm

☐ **B** Increased strength of intercostal muscles   ☐ **D** Increased number of red blood cells

(D) 3 Which of the following is not a benefit of a cool down? **(1 mark)**

☐ **A** Aids the removal of lactic acid

☐ **B** Prevents injury

☐ **C** Aids the removal of carbon dioxide

☐ **D** Helps bring the heart rate and breathing rate slowly back down

(G) 4 Which of the following is an immediate effect of exercise on the cardiovascular system? **(1 mark)**

☐ **A** Increased heart rate   ☐ **C** Increased capillarisation

☐ **B** Increased breathing rate   ☐ **D** Increased oxygen debt

(D) 5 Which of the following statements is correct regarding redistribution of blood flow during exercise? **(1 mark)**

☐ **A** Vasoconstriction is the narrowing of blood vessels supplying the working muscles

☐ **B** Vasoconstriction is the widening of blood vessels supplying the working muscles

☐ **C** Vasodilation is the narrowing of blood vessels supplying the digestive system

☐ **D** Vasodilation is the widening of blood vessels supplying the working muscles

(G) 6 Read the statements and decide which is correct – A, B, C or D. **(1 mark)**

☐ **A** Beta blockers speed up the heart

☐ **B** Beta blockers increase the number of red blood cells

☐ **C** Diuretics can be used to remove other drugs from the body

☐ **D** Diuretics slow down the heart beat

Exam skills: short answer questions

C   1   Describe how to calculate the correct target zone for an endurance athlete.   **(3 marks)**

....

....

....

C   2   Name an appropriate fitness test to measure power **and** describe the test procedure.

Fitness test: ....   **(1 mark)**

Test procedure: ....   **(3 marks)**

....

....

B   3   Explain whether the shot putt is an aerobic or an anaerobic activity.   **(2 marks)**

....

....

D   4   When planning his PEP, Eddie applied the principle of progressive overload.

Describe the principle of progressive overload and state why it is necessary to include in your PEP.   **(2 marks)**

....

....

C   5   Outline an example of how Eddie might have applied progressive overload in his PEP, if he wanted to improve his muscular endurance.   **(2 marks)**

....

....

B   6   SMART targets are set to make training more successful. Explain what the letter M represents and why it should be applied.   **(2 marks)**

....

....

Exam skills: extended answers 1

A 1* Despite being banned substances, there are a number of different performance-enhancing drugs available to sports performers should they choose to use them.

Evaluate the benefits of EPO and diuretics on performance in endurance and power events.

(6 marks)

> Remember, when you see an asterisk next to a question, it means that the quality of your written work will also be assessed in this question. This only happens with extended answer questions.

....

....

....

....

....

....

....

....

....

....

....

....

....

....

....

....

....

....

....

....

Exam skills: extended answers 2

A

1* Mr Clifford is training the school football team and has designed a weight training programme for the team to follow.

Discuss whether weight training would be the most appropriate choice of training method for the football team.

(6 marks)

> Remember, when you see an asterisk next to a question, it means that the quality of your written work will be assessed in this question.

....

....

....

....

....

....

....

....

....

....

....

....

....

....

....

....

....

....

....

....

....

Edexcel publishes official Sample Assessment Material on its website. This Practice Exam Paper has been written to help you practise what you have learned and may not be representative of a real exam paper.

Practice Exam Paper

GCSE Physical Education

Paper 1

Time: 1 hour 30 minutes

Instructions to candidates

- Use blue or black ink.

- Answer **ALL** questions.

- Questions labelled with an **asterisk** (*) are ones where the quality of your written communication will be assessed.

Answer **ALL** questions

For each part of question 1, choose an answer, A, B, C or D, and put a cross in the box ☒.

Mark only one answer for each question. If you change your mind about an answer, put a line through the box ☒ and then mark your new answer with a cross ☒.

1 (a) Which of the following is a correct statement about self-esteem? **(1 mark)**

☐ **A** It means self-centred, a player who does not pass in a game

☐ **B** It is a social benefit of exercise

☐ **C** It can be achieved by becoming better at sport

☐ **D** It happens after a losing streak when you play team games

(b) Which of the following is a key influence on participation from the image category of key influences? **(1 mark)**

☐ **A** Role models

☐ **B** Gender

☐ **C** Perceived status of the activity

☐ **D** Media coverage

(c) Which of the following is the correct definition of fitness? **(1 mark)**

☐ **A** A form of physical activity designed to bring about training adaptations

☐ **B** A lifestyle that contributes positively to physical, social and mental health

☐ **C** The ability to use voluntary muscles many times without tiring

☐ **D** The ability to meet the demands of the environment

(d) Which of the following principles of training is not concerned with injury reduction? **(1 mark)**

☐ **A** Progressive overload

☐ **B** Specificity

☐ **C** Individual differences

☐ **D** Rest and recovery

(e) Which of the following is a correct statement about the redistribution of blood flow during physical activity? **(1 mark)**

☐ **A** It increases the amount of blood flowing to the digestive system

☐ **B** It increases the amount of blood allowed to circulate in the body

☐ **C** It increases the amount of blood flowing to the working muscles

☐ **D** It increases blood flow to the working muscles and digestive system

(f) Which of the following states could be due to additional muscle rather than fat? **(1 mark)**

☐ **A** Overweight

☐ **B** Overfat

☐ **C** Obese

☐ **D** Anorexic

(g) Which of the following is an immediate effect of exercise on the cardiovascular system? **(1 mark)**

☐ **A** Increased breathing rate

☐ **B** Increased heart rate

☐ **C** Increased tidal volume

☐ **D** Increased capillarisation

(h) Which of the following statements is correct in relation to oxygen debt? **(1 mark)**

☐ **A** It is the amount of oxygen owed during exercise

☐ **B** It occurs due to a build up of lactic acid

☐ **C** It is caused by anaerobic respiration and is paid back after exercise

☐ **D** It only occurs in aerobic events lasting more than 5 minutes

(i) Which statement best describes the impact of the use of anabolic steroids? **(1 mark)**

☐ **A** It increases oxygen carrying capacity of the blood

☐ **B** It increases ability to train harder

☐ **C** It increases viscosity of the blood

☐ **D** It decreases the chance of other drugs being detected

(j) Which of the following correctly identifies the movement possibilities at a hinge joint? **(1 mark)**

☐ **A** Flexion, extension, adduction, abduction

☐ **B** Abduction, adduction

☐ **C** Abduction, adduction, rotation

☐ **D** Flexion, extension

(Total 10 marks)

2 Describe a possible impact of serotonin on an individual and their willingness to participate in physical activity. **(3 marks)**

....

....

....

....

....

....

3 Apart from a good knowledge of the rules, identify another quality an official would need **and** outline why this quality is necessary. **(3 marks)**

....

....

....

....

....

....

4 Using an example, describe how initiatives can contribute to the development of healthy lifestyles. **(3 marks)**

....

....

....

....

....

....

5 The performers in **Figure 1** and **Figure 2** require high levels of health-related exercise and skill-related fitness to be the best in their activities.

Figure 1 100 m sprinter

Figure 2 Hurdler

(a) Identify **one** component of health-related exercise that both performers will utilise to achieve success in their event. **(1 mark)**

....

(b) Explain how this component of health-related exercise is used in each event.   **(2 marks)**

Sprinter:...

....

....

Sprint hurdler:...

....

(c) Identify an aspect of skill-related fitness that is more relevant to the hurdler and explain your choice. **(3 marks)**

Aspect of skill-related fitness:

....

Explanation:

....

....

....

....

....

(Total 6 marks)

6 Coaches will measure the fitness of their performers using a range of fitness tests.

In the table:

- Identify the component of health-related exercise or skill-related fitness being measured.

- Name an activity where performers of this activity would find the test useful.

Use a different activity for each test. **(6 marks)**

Fitness test	Component of health-related exercise or skill-related fitness being measured	Activity where performers of this activity would find the test useful
Harvard step test		
Standing broad jump		
Ruler drop test		

7 (a) The table below lists the required components of a balanced diet.

Fats	Vitamins	Carbohydrates	Fibre
Water	Protein	Minerals	

Place the relevant components into the correct box below.

Note that not all components will be placed. **(3 marks)**

Macronutrients

Micronutrients

(b) Explain the link between diet, exercise and health. **(4 marks)**

....

....

....

....

....

....

....

8 Identify **three** different risks and the preventative measures that may be taken, that are associated with team games such as hockey and rugby. **(3 marks)**

....

....

....

....

....

9 Identify **two** factors that have an effect on blood pressure. **(2 marks)**

....

....

10 (a) The table below lists some of the responses given by Year 10 students when asked what the effects of exercise are on the respiratory system.

Increased lung capacity	Increased lactic acid	Antagonistic action between lungs and alveoli	
Hypertrophy of the lungs	Increased oxygen debt	Increased depth of breathing	Increased vital capacity

Choose the correct responses and place each of the effects of exercise on the respiratory system into the correct box below. **(3 marks)**

Immediate effect on the respiratory system	Effect of regular participation on the respiratory system

(b) Explain the effect of smoking on the alveoli-gaseous exchange. **(2 marks)**

....

....

(c) Identify two health risks to the respiratory system associated with smoking. **(2 marks)**

....

....

11 Label the location of the quadriceps and pectorals on **Figure 3** and then explain their function below. **(4 marks)**

Figure 3

Quadriceps: ....

....

Pectorals: ....

....

12 One of the functions of the skeleton is to provide protection. Describe, giving an example, how the skeleton provides protection during physical activity. **(2 marks)**

....

....

....

....

13 Jordan's PE Department regularly invites coaches of less well-known sporting activities to come to the school and run taster sessions for the students in Years 7, 8 and 9 on a Wednesday afternoon.

(a) Identify a physical **and** social benefit to the students of this initiative. **(2 marks)**

Physical: ....

Social: ....

(b) How will this initiative help to increase participation in these sports? **(1 mark)**

....

....

(c) What level of the participation pyramid will the Year 7 students be placed at if they have never tried these sports before? **(1 mark)**

....

....

(d) Identify **two** agencies the school could go to, if they wanted help to increase participation in these sports. **(2 marks)**

....

....

To raise additional funding, the school is thinking of making these sessions available to parents on a Saturday morning.

(e) Considering the term balanced competition, why would the school run the sessions on a Saturday rather than mixing the parents with the students during the Wednesday sessions. **(1 mark)**

....

....

(f) What type of questionnaire should the school use with each of the parents, before allowing them to participate, and why should they use it? **(2 marks)**

....

....

....

....

(g) At the start of each session, a coach always uses a warm up. State **three** reasons why you should warm up before physical activity. **(3 marks)**

....

....

....

....

....

....

(Total 12 marks)

14* Discuss how physical activity may impact on physical fitness and mental health.

....

....

....

....

....

....

....

....

....

....

....

(Total 6 marks)

15* Discuss the long-term training effects of regular participation in physical activity on
the cardiovascular system, and why those effects are important to performance in
endurance events. **(Total 6 marks)**

....

....

....

....

....

....

....

....

....

....

....

Answers

The following pages contain examples of answers that could be made to the questions throughout the workbook and practice exam paper. In many cases these are not the only correct answers.

1. Health and physical activity

1 Social, physical and mental
2 B
3 Make friends with other people of a similar age and with similar interests; to help maintain their health.

2. Mental benefits of an active lifestyle

1 C
2 They would be playing in a team against other teams. They could also be fighting for their place in the team.
3 (a) Mental; (b) Aesthetic; (c) Serotonin: feel good

3. Mental and physical benefits

1 It can relieve stress. It can increase your self-esteem. It can provide a physical challenge.
2 Physical benefit 1: It can lead to weight loss which is good if you are overweight. Link to mental benefit: Can improve self-esteem if you are happier with your healthier weight.
Physical benefit 2: It can improve physical health. Link to mental benefit: Can relieve stress if you are not worried about your physical health.

4. Fitness benefits of an active lifestyle

1 (a) Graham's mum – wants to lose weight as she is becoming overfat.
(b) John – wants to increase muscle mass so not so thin.
2 Improve cardiovascular fitness through regular aerobic activity so they can maintain high level of performance throughout the game. Improve muscular endurance of legs and arms due to regular additional demands made on them by training, allowing them to continue to work well for longer during matches.

5. Health benefits of an active lifestyle

1 (a) Less likely to suffer from osteoporosis; less likely to become obese.
(b) Less likely to suffer from osteoporosis due to increased bone strength as a result of regular weight-bearing exercise. Less likely to become obese due to additional use of calories during exercise.

6. Social benefits of an active lifestyle

1 Making new friends through meeting new people at club. Learning to cooperate with others through playing with others and working with them to become a better team.
2 The children will need to learn how to play with each other, and take it in turns to bowl and therefore they will develop cooperation skills. Whilst taking part in the activity they will also make new friends by socialising with others.
3 By joining a club and swimming and running with others Desmond would come in to contact with other people, through mixing socially others and develop friendships he would improve his social health.

7. Key influences: people

1 Parents, siblings (brothers or sisters), aunts and uncles.
2 Peers, parents, sisters.
3 (a) Role models (b) Peers (c) Family

8. Key influences: image

1 Radio; Sports channels on satellite television
2 'most of the group opted for snowboarding as they thought it was more modern.'; 'and it being broadcast on every channel.'
3 B

9. Key influences: culture

1 (a) Age (b) Disability (c) Gender
2 (a) Age (b) Disability (c) Race (d) Gender

10. Key influences: resources

1 Time
2 (a) Access (b) Access (c) Location (d) Availability

11. Key influences: health and wellbeing and socio-economic

1 'since his operation he could no longer cover the court'; 'playing golf because he liked the status of the activity'; 'missed the last four sessions due to a very bad cold.'; 'he cannot afford the fees.'
2 C
3 Cost

12. Roles and required qualities

1 Good people management skills, good communication skills, good planning skills
2 (a) Performing, coaching
(b) To give people options so they can find something they want to become involved in. Also if their tastes change due to age or injury for example they can change their role but still remain involved in physical activity.
3 Squash – you can become involved in squash as a player, official (marker) and coach. Anyone can play squash as a performer, but the number of people who play on court does decrease as people get older as it is a very energetic game. If people still want to be part of squash they can become a marker and record the score during club matches. This is a sedentary role but you need to know the rules well to do it properly. Even if you enjoy playing, if you want to help others get better you could coach. Many coaches will coach a junior squad on a Saturday morning.

13. Sports participation pyramid 1

1 (a) Participation (b) Foundation (c) Participation
2 The bottom of the pyramid where the greatest number of people will be for any activity. This is where people are introduced to a new sport, maybe in school PE lessons. It's the first time they try something, so people will learn basic skills during this stage.
3 Decide they want to continue with the activity and use their free time to do so. They could join a club and play for a team, but this would be at a low level.

14. Sports participation pyramid 2

1 (a) Performance (b) Performance (c) Elite
2 This is where you really start to develop your skills and get good at the activity. You have regular coaching to help you improve and play at competitive level. You're not quite at national level but will play for a high division or regional level.
3 Continue to improve skills as a result of hard work and coaching so that you are selected to play at national or international level.

15. Initiatives and their common purposes

1 Increase participation; educate about the need for a healthy active lifestyle
2 Essay question: would need to be well written, address all aspects of the questions and give developed answers. There are many 'correct' ways to answer the question but you should have made reference to the following:
   • discussion of physical, mental and social benefits with examples
   • clear links between initiatives and increased opportunity for activity leading to stated health benefits
   • links between healthy eating and improved health.

16. Agencies

1 Youth Sport Trust; National Governing Bodies
2 (a) Sport England (b) National Governing Bodies
3 National Governing Bodies

17. Health, fitness and exercise

1 Health is physical, social and mental wellbeing and being free from disease. Fitness is having the ability to meet the demands of your environment.
2 Fitness is having the ability to meet the demands of your environment. This means that different people will require different levels of fitness, depending on what they do on a day to day basis. For example, a postman who walks several miles a day delivering mail will need to be fit enough to do this; if he isn't, he can't do his job and therefore will not meet the demands of his environment.
3 Exercise is an activity that we do in order to improve or maintain our health and fitness. If we improve our fitness through regular exercise, this will make us fitter for our activity, which will allow us to perform better. For example, a fitter footballer is less likely to get substituted during a game because their performance won't suffer as the game progresses.

18. Health, fitness and exercise and a balanced healthy lifestyle

1 (a) Exercise (b) Fitness (c) Health
2 You can start anywhere on the diagram, each factor potentially impacts on the next. If you exercise you can increase your fitness. This in turn can lead to an increase in health. Regular exercise, good health and fitness will help to achieve a healthy balanced lifestyle. It is important that the exercise forms a balanced part of the lifestyle otherwise ill health can result.

19. Cardiovascular fitness and muscular endurance

1 C
2 (a) Oxygen, exercise, tiring
   (b) Heart, muscles, quality
   (c) Coronary heart disease
3 Muscular endurance involves repeated contraction of specific muscles during an activity without tiring, whereas cardiovascular fitness means the ability to exercise the entire body for long periods of time without tiring. Therefore both need to work for long periods of time without tiring, but one is about specific muscles while the other is about the whole body.

20. Muscular strength, flexibility and body composition

1

The percentage of body weight, which is fat, muscle and bone	Body composition
The range of movement possible at a joint	Flexibility
The ability to exercise the entire body for long periods of time without tiring	Cardiovascular fitness
The amount of force a muscle can exert against a resistance	Muscular strength
The ability to use voluntary muscles many times without getting tired	Muscular endurance

21. Agility, balance and coordination

1 D
2 (a) Agility, skill-related fitness
   (b) Skill-related fitness, balance
3 (a) Agility is the ability to change the position of the body quickly and to control the movement of the whole body. Coordination is the ability to use two or more body parts together.
   (b) Changing the position of the body quickly with control means that movements must be coordinated. Without good coordination it would be very difficult to develop good agility.

Answers

22. Power, reaction time and speed 1

1

The ability to do strength performances quickly	Power
The differential rate at which an individual is able to perform a movement or cover a distance in a period of time	Speed
The time between the presentation of a stimulus and the onset of a movement	Reaction time
The ability to use two or more body parts together	Coordination
The ability to retain the body's centre of mass (gravity) above the base of support with reference to static (stationary), or dynamic (changing) conditions of movement, shape and orientation	Balance
The ability to change the position of the body quickly and to control the movement of the whole body	Agility

23. Effects of cardiovascular fitness and muscular endurance

1 A

2 **(a)** Cardiovascular fitness **(b)** Cardiovascular fitness **(c)** Muscular endurance

3 Cardiovascular fitness is used to supply additional oxygen to the working muscles so that the tennis player can keep moving effectively on the court to get to and return the ball even after playing for more than an hour. Muscular endurance is used for the repeated muscle contractions over a long period of time without tiring; this means the arms can keep generating enough strength to play hard shots, making it more difficult for the opponent to return.

4 Although a marathon runner may use speed for a sprint finish or to get past an opponent, cardiovascular fitness is more important as it allows them to supply additional oxygen to the body and maintain performance for a long time – speed is only used for a very short time. The marathon is a long event taking hours to complete. In order to have sufficient energy to keep working for this amount of time, oxygen is needed; without high cardiovascular fitness the runner would need to slow down or stop.

24. Effects of muscular strength, flexibility and body composition

1 C

2

Performer	How flexibility is used in activity
Sprinter	At the hip to get a long stride therefore using as few strides as possible to complete the race in a quicker time
Javelin thrower	At the shoulder to get full extension so they can throw further
Gymnast in a floor routine	At the hips doing the splits so the correct shape is achieved without injury or loss of points

3. Essay question would need to be well written, balanced, in sentences (not bullet points) and have a conclusion. However, the content could include the following:

Body composition is important to all performers as they need an appropriate ratio of body fat to muscle for their activity.

However, some might say body composition is not important to performers because there are examples of under-weight and overfat people who manage very well in their activity.

A gymnast needs to support their body weight and have high levels of flexibility, therefore they will need a relatively low percentage of body fat so there is minimal additional weight to lift and flexibility is not reduced. For example, too much body fat or muscle would hinder a performer doing the splits. Gymnasts need a high ratio of muscle to body fat to allow them to perform tumbling routines.

Games players vary depending on the position or game they are playing. For example, a rugby player would need a higher ratio of muscle to give them the strength to fight off tackles.

In conclusion, better performers tend to have an appropriate ratio of body fat to muscle for their activity. If they have too much or too little body fat or muscle, they will not be able to perform as well.

25. Effects of agility, balance and coordination

1 A

2 **(a)** Agility **(b)** Coordination

3 Squash players need agility to change direction quickly to reach the ball. Footballers need agility to quickly dodge around the opposition when dribbling the ball.

4 Coordination is important in hockey and trampolining. In hockey you need hand-eye coordination to manipulate the hockey stick in to the correct position to stop an oncoming ball. In trampolining you need to be able to coordinate arms and legs during a straight bounce so that your body remains balanced and you can maintain a central position on the trampoline.

5 Balance is needed during flight to maintain body shape and centre of gravity in correct position, therefore increasing the chance of clearing the bar.

26. Power, reaction time and speed 2

1

Player	Example of use of speed by performer in activity	Impact of speed on performance
Rugby player	To sprint past opponents with the ball	To score a try without getting stopped
Sprinter	To run as fast as they can to the finish line	To run faster and beat opponents
Long jumper	To run fast in the run-up before the jump	To achieve a greater distance in the jump.

105

2 (a) Component 1 – Speed; Component 2 – Power.
   (b) Speed is used to bring the arm through quickly to get a good distance on the throw and power is used to generate more force so the javelin goes further.

27. PAR-Q and fitness tests

1 Is there any history of coronary heart disease in your family? Yes / No; Are you taking any prescription drugs or medication? Yes / No

2 Look for the area of weakness based on the ratings. It looks like Michael has very poor flexibility so I would include more flexibility work in his PEP.

28. Fitness tests 1

1 (a) Use a 400 m track and run around the track as many times as possible in 12 minutes. Measure the distance you have covered in the 12 minutes and rate your fitness using rating tables.
   (b) To measure cardiovascular fitness, when re-testing fitness after following a training programme, if running a test outside with a large group.

2 Harvard step test because this way the whole group would be involved in the testing process at the same time, with half completing the test while the other half record heart rate values. The treadmill test would take a long time to complete unless there were sufficient treadmills for one each.

29. Fitness tests 2

1 (a) Figure 1 – hand grip test, Figure 2 – sit and reach test
   (b) Figure 1 – measures strength, Figure 2 – measures flexibility
   (c) Figure 1 – rock climbing Figure 2 – gymnastics
   (d) A

30. Fitness tests 3

1 (a) 30-metre sprint is run in a straight line but weave around obstacles in the Illinois agility test.
   (b) Agility is the ability to change body position quickly so the Illinois agility test includes something that measures this, i.e. the swerving, but the 30-metre sprint test just measures speed between A and B so only need to run in a straight line.
   (c) (i) 100 m; football
       (ii) 100 m: because they are clearly fast over 30 m, they may also be fast over 100 m. Sprinting races are won by the fastest therefore they could win.
       Football: speed over a short distance is really helpful to beat your opponent to the ball. Therefore this would make them more valuable than a slower player in certain positions.

2 (a) Illinois agility run (b) Basketball

31. Fitness tests 4

1 (a) Figure 1 – standing broad jump test
   (b) Figure 2 – Sargent Jump test
   (c) Stand still, with toes behind a line. Jump forwards as far as you can, using a two footed take-off. Measure the distance from the start line to the landing point.

32. Fitness tests 5

1 (a) Ruler drop test

   (b) Student F as they had the best reaction time. This means they will be able to make decisions quicker than their team mates about when and where to move based on the stimulus. In goal you have to make very quick decisions when trying to save a shot and the outcome is more critical when you are in goal if you make a slow decision, so you need someone with good reaction time in that position.

2 Standing stork test – competitive swimmers need to be able to stand still on the blocks to reduce the chance of a false start. The ruler drop test measures reaction time – they need a good reaction time at the start of the race to get away from the blocks. Three ball juggle – measures coordination, and good coordination is needed in swimming to time the movement of the arms with the legs, but the action in juggling is very different from the action in the pool.

33. Principles of training: progressive overload

1 (a) If you looked at the plans for each session you would see an increase in intensity between the first session and the last. If there was a gradual increase between the sessions this would be progressive overload. For example, if in week 1 the person did 20 sit-ups, 25 in week 2, 30 in week 3, this would be progressive overload.
   (b) If you looked at the results of the first set of tests and compared these to the second, you should see an increase in fitness test scores in the tests that related to the areas where progressive overload had been applied. For example, if in test 1 the person was ranked very poor in a strength test but then when re-tested achieved a higher ranking this could be due to the use of progressive overload when lifting weights.

2 A

34. Principles of training: specificity

1 (a) Interval (b) Continuous
   (c) Weight training (d) Fartlek

2 Footballer would focus on varying intensity within fartlek training, for example, short sprint maximum intensity then a period of jogging for recovery to match movement on pitch. Cross country runner would focus on change of terrain within fartlek training, for example, running up and down hills, on the road and through the forest.

35. Principles of training: individual differences / rest and recovery

1 C

2 Rest and recovery

3 The principle of individual differences means that you make sure your training is tailor made to focus on your needs rather than just the needs of the sport. If you focus on your weaknesses and improve these, your performance will improve. For example, if I improved my cardiovascular fitness, I would be able to maintain the quality of my performance in matches for longer.

4 To make sure that you have sufficient rest so you have opportunity for fitness adaptations to take place. Without this you will not improve.

36. Principles of training: FITT principle and reversibility

1 F – frequency, by making sure they exercise regularly so the training can have an impact.
I – intensity, by making sure they work hard enough to cause adaptations to improve fitness.
T – time, by making sure they work for long enough in a session to make the body work harder.
T – type, by making sure their training matches the needs of the sport. If not, they may improve some aspects of fitness but if not used in the sport this will not improve performance.

2 Student B because his is the only heart rate that increases during the eight weeks.

37. Value of goal setting and SMART targets

1 Helps you to plan your training by giving specific focus. Helps you to develop your ability by focusing on weaknesses. Helps you maintain training by motivating you to continue to work towards the goal or target.

2 To move up to the second team by the second half of the season.

3 (a) Decrease time to 14 s
   (b) Increase high jump to 1 m 55 cm
   (c) Get into the first team
   (d) Increase total goals scored over next six games to 12
   (e) Increase their personal best tariff score to 5.0

38. SMART targets

1 (a) Not achievable – to take almost 2 seconds off of their 100 m time within two weeks would be too difficult to achieve. It may be possible over a longer period.
   (b) Not achievable – too big a jump from 3rd to 1st place in a competition where there will be very good performers as at county level.
   (c) Not achievable – a huge increase in number of goals needing to be scored; would need to score at least 3 goals per match.
   (d) Not achievable – an increase of 1.5 to achieve a perfect score would be very difficult, especially by their next competition.

2 Play for the second team by the end of next season.

39. Interval training

1 (a) Interval training has breaks built into the session (to allow recovery) whereas continuous training does not.
   (b) Although normally used for anaerobic events, interval training can be adapted for use by endurance athletes. For example, rather than having short periods of work, the work intervals can be made longer and the recovery periods could be active recovery rather than complete rest.
   (c) 100 m sprinter and long jumper
   (d) Circuit training – to make it more like interval training, there would be a set period of work on each station, for example 45 seconds, followed by a set period of rest, for example 30 seconds, before moving on to the next station. This should allow the performer sufficient time for recovery so they can still work at a high intensity.

40. Continuous training

1 Marathon runner, hockey player, long distance swimmer

2 C

3 Continuous training would be seen as a challenge by many if new to training, to have the mental willpower to continue to work. If achieved this provides mental benefits of satisfaction and increased self-esteem. Many people will also complete continuous training in a club and run with others, talking and socialising with other runners therefore improving their social health. Physical health is also improved as continuous training normally involves weight-bearing exercises like running; this can strengthen bones and reduce the chance of health issues occurring, such as osteoporosis. As continuous training is aerobic, it can also help with weight control if there is a need to reduce weight to reduce weight-related health issues.

4 A and C

41. Fartlek training

1 (a) This area would be ideal as it meets the requirements of fartlek training by providing a variety of terrains, which would lead to changes in speed. For example, there is a hill so you could practice running up and down hill, allowing you to vary how hard you are working, as it is hard to run up hill so you would vary your speed. The stream, gravel track, woods and grass area are all different types of surface to run on, so give the opportunity to practice on different terrains.
   (b) Cross country runner, games player
   (c) Cardiovascular fitness and muscular endurance.

42. Circuit training

1 (a) and (b)

Station	(a) Possible circuit	(b) Component of fitness
1	Shuttle runs	Speed
2	Sit-ups	Muscular endurance
3	Bench astrides	Power
4	Seated dips	Muscular strength
5	Jumping jacks	Power
6	Obliques	Muscular endurance

   (c) It is a good idea to alternate muscle groups being worked to allow the muscles time for recovery before having to work hard again.

43. Weight training

1 (a) Weight training involves working with a resistance; this can be free weights or fixed weights. You would normally complete a number of repetitions per set and a number of sets, for example 12 repetitions per set and 3 sets. Typical exercises would be a biceps curl and a leg press.
   (b) Muscular strength and muscular endurance.
   (c) The amount a person lifts can be altered to match their needs. The stronger the individual, the heavier the weights they can lift. Performers could use the 1RM (one rep max) to find how

much they can lift and then lift a percentage of
that, depending on which aspect of strength they
wish to increase.
  (d) An endurance athlete would lift lighter weights
      but do more reps; a power athlete would lift
      heavier weights with fewer reps.

44. Cross training
1 (a) A mixture of training, for example it could
      include running, swimming and cycling as a way
      of keeping fit, rather than just using one type of
      training like running.
  (b) Performers who need to be fit for a variety
      of activities, for example people who enjoy
      competing in triathlons.
  (c) It can keep you motivated to train as you are
      not doing the same thing all the time. It can help
      reduce overuse injuries as you are not repeating
      the same exercises all of the time, for example,
      rather than road running every day you might
      only road run once a week reducing the wear
      and tear on your joints. It increases your social
      network and therefore maintains or improves
      social health as you meet different groups
      of people when taking part in the different
      activities. You can train in a wide variety of areas
      of fitness across all of the sessions, for example,
      cardiovascular fitness when running; muscular
      strength in a weights session and power in a
      circuit session.

45. Exercise session: warm up
1 (a) Row 1 – Pulse raise e.g. jog around court,
      running forwards, backwards, sideways. Row 2
      – Stretching, e.g. hamstring stretch. Row 3 –
      Drills specific to your activity e.g. for a squash
      player, fast paced movement to and from the 'T',
      shadowing action of playing a shot in each corner.
  (b) The final phase of the warm up should relate
      to the activity you are about to take part in,
      therefore the performer should choose something
      that relates to their activity. Different activities
      will have different drills associated with them.
      For example, a badminton player would perform
      drills involving movement around the court and
      the practising of badminton strokes, whereas a
      footballer would use a football to practise skills
      they would use in the game.
  (c) To reduce chance of pulling a muscle. To increase
      blood flow, increasing oxygen availability.

46. Exercise session: main session and cool down
1 (a) Run a cool-down.
  (b) Two phases to a cool-down – there should be
      a slow reduction in the intensity of activity, for
      example jogging reducing intensity to a slow jog
      or walk. After this the performer should stretch
      the muscles that have been in use during the
      main session, for example runners would focus
      on the leg muscles.
  (c) The intensity of the activity should gradually
      decrease.
  (d) To slowly return the body to its resting state.
      It will help remove lactic acid, replenish oxygen
      stores, reduce the body temperature.

47. Exercise session: endurance
1 (a) Circuit training, continuous training, fartlek
      training
  (b) Circuit training – you would include stations to
      improve muscular endurance and cardiovascular
      fitness, e.g. squats, abdominal curls, press ups,
      skipping, dorsal raises, triceps dip, working
      aerobically to complete a set number rather than
      for a set period of time, therefore improving their
      cardiovascular fitness and muscular endurance.
      Fartlek – focus on jogging rather than speed,
      although some sprinting can be included. For
      example, jog for 12 minutes at 60% maximum
      heart rate followed by a series of short sprints
      with a short walk in-between to allow recovery
      from the sprint.

48. Exercise session: power
1 (a) Circuit training, weight training, interval training
  (b) Circuit training – you would select stations for
      strength and speed, e.g. squats and press ups,
      working anaerobically for a set period of time
      therefore increasing power.
      Weight training – the performer could work
      anaerobically to complete a series of repetitions
      and sets, for example three sets of six repetitions
      at 80% of their 1 rep max, therefore increasing
      power.
  (c) Progressive overload, specificity

49. Heart rates and graphs
1 (a) He can see whether or not his resting heart
      rate decreases. If it does, it is likely that he is
      increasing his fitness. If it does not it could mean
      that his training is not being effective and needs
      changing.
  (b)(i) After two minutes there is an increase in
         heart rate; it would be at this point that
         Martin increases the intensity of the work
         he is doing and therefore needs to increase
         blood flow to aid oxygen delivery.
     (ii) Martin reduced the intensity of the work he
          was doing as the heart rate goes down.
     (iii) Martin had not completely recovered, as his
           heart rate in the 13th minute was still higher
           than his resting heart rate at the start of
           exercise.

50. Setting training target zones
1 The terms relate to level of heart rate during activity.
  There is an upper and lower training threshold
  that we want to keep our heart rate within. The
  section between upper and lower heart rate training
  threshold values is called our target zone. These are
  used to help us train at the correct intensity to bring
  about the improvement in fitness that we need for
  our activity.
2 (a) Maximum heart rate is 220 – sister's age,
      therefore 204 bpm upper limit will be 80% of the
      maximum heart rate. The lower limit will be 60%
      of the maximum heart rate.
  (b) They are training for events that have different
      intensities, one is aerobic, one is anaerobic.
      Therefore they need to train at different
      thresholds to mirror the requirements of their
      activity. Jed will work at a lower training
      threshold than Mike.

51. Requirements of a balanced diet

1 (a) (i) Carbohydrates, fats, proteins, minerals, vitamins, water, fibre

(ii) A = carbohydrates, B = proteins, C = fats

52. Macronutrients

1 D

2 One could be a man, the other a woman. The recommended intake is less for women than men. They could do different sports and therefore have different energy demands.

3 Carbohydrates are used for energy; without sufficient energy we would not be able to be active. Proteins are needed for growth and repair of body cells; without protein we would not be able to repair damaged muscle cells, which would prevent us from remaining active.

53. Micronutrients

1 (a) Something that you should eat that is good for the body (nutrient) that is only needed in small quantities on a daily basis (micro).

(b)

Types of micronutrient		Examples of each type of micronutrient
1	Vitamins	e.g. Vitamin C
		e.g. Vitamin D
2	Minerals	e.g. Iron
		e.g. Calcium

(c) Vitamin C can reduce the risk of heart disease if correct quantities taken; vitamin D encourages the absorption of calcium to help strengthen bones; iron is an important part of haemoglobin without sufficient iron could become anaemic and not be able to transport oxygen effectively; calcium is needed for healthy bones, so lack of calcium can lead to osteoporosis.

54. Timing of dietary intake

1 When you are at rest there is greater blood flow to the digestive system, so that the food can be digested properly. When we exercise there is a reduction in blood flow to the digestive system in favour of the muscles that are working. This means that we should not exercise immediately before exercise, otherwise there will not be sufficient blood available to digest our food; we should wait a couple of hours before exercising after eating a large meal.

55. Redistribution of blood flow

1 (a) This is the term for the process when blood flow to different parts of the body is altered. For example, when exercising blood flow to the working muscles increases but blood flow to the digestive system decreases. The redistribution of blood from one area to another is known as blood shunting.

(b) Blood flow reduces through vasoconstriction. This is when the amount of space for the blood to flow through gets smaller therefore less blood can pass through. This is necessary so that there can be additional blood flow to the working muscles.

(c) Increased blood flow to the working muscles means more oxygen is available, allowing more (aerobic) energy for exercise.

56. Mesomorphs

1 Mesomorph

2 (a) High levels of muscle, as seen in the sprinter's arms and legs; wide shoulders as seen in the weight lifter; narrow hips as shown by the weight lifter; low levels of fat as shown by the boxer.

(b) High levels of muscle allow them to produce more power, for example more power to run faster, hit harder, lift more weight; low levels of fat so not carrying unnecessary weight, which would impede performance, for example boxer can make weight with most efficient amount of muscle.

3 Strength; power; speed

57. Ectomorphs and endomorphs

1 (a) Wider hips; narrow shoulders; more likely to store fat.

(b Additional fat will increase the weight of the body; this would give the thrower more mass, which can help to get further distance on the throw due to an increase in momentum.

2 Tall – centre of gravity higher than shorter person, so less distance to lift over bar, therefore can jump higher; tend not to store fat therefore lighter, so less weight to lift over the bar making jump easier.

3 Football goalkeeper; basketball player; netball goal shooter

58. Factors affecting optimum weight

1 Ideal weight for an individual based on certain physiological factors, e.g. height.

2 Your height will affect your optimum weight, the taller you are the more you will weigh. Sex – men tend to have more muscle than women therefore a man of the same height as a woman is likely to weigh more. Bone structure – the more dense your bones the heavier you will be. Muscle girth – the more muscular you are the more you will weigh.

3 Jockeys need to be light therefore they tend to be short compared to other sports performers. In high jumping it is an advantage to be tall, which will increase weight, so high jumpers tend to be tall but with limited muscle girth compared to other performers in other activities.

59. Anorexia and underweight

1 Anorexia is an eating disorder where an individual becomes dangerously underweight.

2 If you don't eat much food you will lack sufficient energy for physical activity. If you are obsessed with exercise this will burn even more calories until you don't have sufficient energy to exercise. If you are tired you would find it difficult to perform to a reasonable standard, or lack motivation to carry out physical work. If you are dehydrated the blood becomes thicker therefore it takes longer for nutrients to reach muscles. You will not be well enough to exercise.

3 Underweight is weighing less than is normal or healthy. If someone is extremely underweight it could be a symptom of anorexia, which is a very serious eating disorder.

60. Overweight, overfat, obese

1 (a) Obese, overfat, overweight

   (b) If you are obese this can lead to a number of health issues, such as Type II diabetes and heart disease, it can also reduce life expectancy. If you are overfat this is still a health issue as this can lead to increased blood pressure and high cholesterol. Being overweight might be nothing to do with having extra fat, you could be overweight because you have dense bones or have a lot of muscle mass, so this need not be dangerous to health at all.

2 Regular activity will use calories that would otherwise be stored in the body. Therefore if you exercise regularly, you will put on less weight than if you didn't exercise at all.

61. Anabolic steroids

1 Increased aggression; acne; low sperm count

2 Sprinters need to develop strength and power whereas long distance runners focus more on muscular endurance. These drugs allow the performer to increase strength and power through appropriate training, making them more relevant to the sprinter.

3 It gives performers an unfair advantage over their competitors by allowing them to train harder and for longer so they can build more muscle and stand a greater chance of winning.

62. Beta blockers

1 Performers in events where they need to be steady and calm may take them, so performers in events that require small accurate movements, for example shooting, are more likely to take these drugs. Other performers in very physical games, for example rugby, would not want to become too relaxed so would not take beta blockers.

2 Poor sleep leading to tiredness and low blood pressure.

3 For some performers they will improve their performance as they reduce the physical effects of anxiety meaning that in events needing precision the performer can be in more control.

4 Archery, diving

63. Diuretics

1 (a) Dehydration occurs because more water is lost from the body than taken in. The loss of water is caused by the diuretic.

   (b) Kidney failure – the performer will need hospital treatment and therefore will not be able to perform.
   Feeling nauseous – if this happens the performer will lose focus on the tasks they are completing; they will be distracted and not be able to carry out essential techniques or skills effectively; for example they could fail to tackle an on-coming opponent or drop a catch therefore performance will suffer.

   (c) Horse racing and boxing – to make the weight limits.

64. Narcotic analgesics

1 (a) Vomiting, loss of concentration

   (b) Excessive vomiting can lead to dehydration.

2 (a) Tennis player who gets injured during a game but has to play in the next round of the tournament in two days time might take them to mask the pain so they can still play.

   (b) Because they encourage people to play with injuries, which puts the player at greater risk of having a long-term injury.

65. Stimulants

1 (a) Increased anxiety, which can lead to depression. Increased aggression can damage social health due to the way you behave towards others.

   (b) Discovery – if found to be taking performance enhancing drugs, competitors will be banned from competing. Depending on the type of stimulant athletes could have a criminal record as these drugs are illegal.

2 Stimulants can cause an increase in aggression. In some sports, like boxing, aggression is a very important quality to have as the boxer needs to be prepared to become involved in a physical fight with another performer, they need to be able to 'attack' their opponent and aggression is needed for this.

66. Peptide hormones

1 EPO is more likely to be taken by the long distance runner because it increases the red blood cell count, which means the long distance runner can carry more oxygen. With more oxygen they can maintain a higher pace in the race for longer as it is used to release energy. It would have the same effect for sprinters, but their race doesn't rely on increased oxygen to complete it, so it doesn't give them the same advantage.

2 Heart failure and increased viscosity of the blood.

67. Recreational drugs

1 (a) Cardiovascular system; respiratory system.

   (b) (i) Performance enhancing drugs are illegal.
      (ii) They will not improve performance therefore will not give an athlete an unfair advantage.

   (c) Smoking can cause lung cancer. This is because the smoke contains carcinogens.

   (d) Alcohol can cause liver damage for example cirrhosis. This is because normal liver tissue is replaced by scar tissue, which causes liver cells to die, making it harder for the liver to function.

68. Reducing risk through personal readiness

1 (a) Judo – bruising by being thrown to the floor by opponent; football – graze / cuts to shins from opponent's studs; high diving – concussion from hitting head on pool side due to mistimed dive; boxing – dislocated jaw from a punch to the face.

   (b) Football – wear shin pads to protect the skin, therefore if kicked the opponent's studs will hit the shin pad, which will soften the blow on Bruno's leg and make it less likely that he will get a cut to the shin.

2 (a) Pulled muscle; (b) Broken tooth; (c) Cuts.

69. Reducing risk through other measures

1 (a) Horse riding – helmet; squash – safety glasses; dance – warm up; skiing – protective padding.

   (b) Helmet – cushions the blow to the head if the rider falls therefore protects the brain from injury; Squash glasses – protect the player from a detached retina as the glasses stop the ball squashing in to the eye; Dance – warming up increases muscle elasticity so less likely to pull a muscle; Skiing – protective padding around pylons so that if a skier skis into them at speed the impact will be reduced by the padding.

70. Cardiovascular system and exercise

1 **(a)** HR = heart rate, SV = stroke volume; cardiac output is the product of HR and SV; this means the amount of blood ejected from the heart per minute.
   (b) Increases due to increase in HR and SV.
   (c) Increased oxygen delivery, so that more oxygen is available for energy release and the performer can work at a greater intensity as required by the activity.
2 C

71. Cardiovascular system: adaptations 1

1 **(a)** A
   (b) Larger muscle wall than B; when we train, our body adapts to the extra work; this means the heart gets stronger.
2 Increased strength of heart therefore reduction in CHD. Drop in resting blood pressure therefore less likely to have a stroke.

72. Cardiovascular system: adaptations 2

1 More efficient recovery so that the participant is ready to perform again sooner.
2 Hockey is an endurance activity. This type of activity is aerobic. The increased number of capillaries will help with an increase in transport of oxygen to the working muscles.
3 **(a)** None
   (b) Cardiac output at rest will be the same regardless of whether trained or not. Although the values for HR and SV may change, the answer to the equation (cardiac output value) remains the same.
4 A

73. Blood pressure and cholesterol

1 Systolic; diastolic
2 Because the heart contracts and relaxes so there is one blood pressure for when heart is contracting – systolic – and one for when the heart relaxes – diastolic.
3 Heart rate increases during exercise. This means more blood is flowing through the blood vessels. Increased blood flow will increase blood pressure.
4 Systolic, because this is the pressure when the heart contracts, therefore blood flow increases compared to when the heart is relaxing.
5 B

74. Respiratory system and exercise

1 **(a)** Increase in breathing rate.
   (b) Increase in oxygen intake and increased removal of carbon dioxide, therefore they can continue to work for longer.
   (c) A
2 Oxygen; oxygen; after; above; rest
3 It could make performance worse, for example, if I was a marathon runner I would not be able to get enough oxygen to perform well as there would be a reduction in oxygen uptake by the red blood cells.

75. Respiratory system: adaptations

1 **(a)** Increased removal of carbon dioxide from the body and increased vital capacity.
   (b) (i) Long distance runner

   (ii) Alveoli are the site where gaseous exchange takes place in the lungs. If there are more places for gas exchange to take place, more oxygen can be extracted from air. With more oxygen the performer can improve their cardiovascular fitness and their performance.
   (c) (i) A sprinter
   (ii) They work anaerobically therefore performance is not dependent on good aerobic fitness.
2 Vital capacity is the maximum amount of air that can be forcibly exhaled after breathing in.

76. Antagonistic muscle pairs: biceps and triceps

1 Biceps
2 **(a)** Skeletal muscles work together to provide movement – while one muscle contracts another relaxes, causing the bone they are attached to move.
   (b) Triceps
   (c) When the biceps contracts the triceps relaxes. This allows the runner to bend the arm at the elbow. To take the arm back again, the biceps relaxes and the triceps contracts.
   (d) It allows the sprinter to 'pump' the arms, adding more power, which allows him to run faster.
   (e) Flexion and extension of the arm at the elbow.

77. Antagonistic muscle pairs: quadriceps and hamstrings

1 **(a) (i)** Quadriceps
   (ii) Extend the leg at the knee.
   (b) Follow through with the leg after taking a shot at goal in football; performing a pike jump in trampolining; during the drive phase when running.
   (c) (i) Hamstrings.
   (ii) To flex the leg at the knee.
   (iii) In gymnastics when tucking the knees up to increase speed of rotation in a tumbling move.

78. Gluteals, gastrocnemius and deltoid

1 Buttocks; extending; shoulder; arm
2 **(a)** Deltoid;
   (b) Gastrocnemius
3 Shoulder action during butterfly stroke; taking the racquet back in preparation to hit a ball in tennis.
4 Allows the performer to extend her leg upwards to form the balance.

79. Trapezius, latissimus dorsi, pectorals and abdominals

1 **(a) (i)** Pectorals – upper chest; abdominals – centre of torso
   (ii) Pectorals will be used to move the racket across the body when playing a forehand. Abdominals will be used to flex the trunk when he bends to play a shot.
2 A = Latissimus dorsi; B = Trapezius; A is responsible for adducting the upper arm at the shoulder. B is responsible for rotating the scapular towards the spine.

80. The muscular system and exercise

1 Isotonic is when the muscle contracts and movement occurs; isometric is when the muscle contracts and no movement occurs.
2 Isometric; isometric; isotonic; isometric
3 Increase in temperature; increased demand for oxygen; increased production of carbon dioxide
4 Increased carbon dioxide levels due to carbon dioxide being made by the body because during exercise we need more energy so the process of releasing more energy also means more carbon dioxide is produced as a bi-product.

81. The muscular system: adaptations

1 C
2 Increased size and strength of the muscles would help them gain more power and therefore sprint faster.
3 Increase in myoglobin
4 Increase in muscle size
5 C

82. Functions of the skeletal system

1 (a) The skull protects the brain if hit in the head by a hockey stick. The ribcage protects the heart and lungs if hit in the chest by a golf ball.
  (b) Function: support; example: keeps body in an upright position when running. Function: movement; example: works with muscles to move arm when playing tennis.
2 Figure 1 – the skeleton supports the boxer by keeping him in an upright position to he can maintain the correct stance. Figure 2 – The ribcage protects the heart and lungs if hit in the chest by a cricket ball.
3 Bones; levers; movement; muscles

83. What you need to know about joints

1 (a) The place where two or more bones meet.
  (b) Joint A – elbow joint; hinge joint. Joint B – shoulder joint; ball and socket joint. Joint C – hip joint; ball and socket joint. Joint D – knee joint; hinge joint.

84. Range of movement at joints 1

1 (a) Reduction of the angle at a joint, for example, the arm at the elbow in preparation for a chest pass,
  (b) Increase the angle at a joint, for example keeping the arm straight when trying to block the ball in volleyball.
2 (a) Figure 1 – knees; hips. Figure 2 – elbows; hips; knees.
  (b) Figure 3 – elbows; hips; knees. Figure 4 – elbow.

85. Range of movement at joints 2

1 (a) Movement of a limb away from the body, for example the movement of the arm at the shoulder as it moves away from the body and reaches towards the floor in a cartwheel.
  (b) Circular movement at a joint, for example overarm bowling action in cricket.
2 (a) Figure 1 (b) C

86. The skeletal system and exercise

1 (a)(i) Walking (ii) Aerobics; tennis
  (b) Weight bearing activities make your body work against gravity; in other words, support your own body weight, whereas non-weight bearing

means you have help supporting body weight, like sitting in a boat.
  (c) Increased bone density; stronger bones; reduced chance of osteoporosis; better posture
2 A
3 Less chance of fractures

87. Potential injuries: fractures

1 (a) Fracture
  (b) A = simple; B = compound; C = stress; D = greenstick
  (c) Injury A – a small crack forms in the bone. This can be an overuse injury from running on hard surfaces without appropriate rest.
  (d) The bone breaks but does not come through the skin. This could be caused in games like football where the player falls awkwardly, twisting the ankle violently.
2 B

88. Potential injuries: joint injuries

1 A
2 Overuse
3 The bone ends that meet at a joint get separated.
4 Mistimed catch of ball in netball so force of pass bends finger back.
5 C
6 Inflamed tendons

89. Potential injuries: sprains and torn cartilage

1

	Injury	Description	Symptom
(a)	Torn cartilage	Small tears appear in the cartilage at the end of the bones	Pain
(b)	Sprain	The joint moves out of position when the ligaments get stretched	Swelling

2 (a) B
  (b) R = Rest, I = Ice, C = Compression, E = Elevation

90. Exam skills: multiple choice questions

1 A 2 D 3 B 4 A 5 D 6 C

91. Exam skills: short answer questions

1 220 minus the age of the athlete, 60% of the total, 80% per cent of the total.
2 Standing broad jump. Stand both feet together and jump forwards from a stationary position. Measure the distance and compare to national ratings chart.
3 Anaerobic as it is a short explosive activity that does not require oxygen.
4 Progressive overload gradually increasing the intensity of the workload. This increases fitness but avoids injury.
5 Week 1 he could complete 3 sets of 8 reps of 5 kgs. Week 3 he could complete 3 sets of 10 reps of 5 kgs.
6 Measureable – to make it possible to tell if the target is achieved.

92. Exam skills: extended answers 1

This is an example of a good answer. Remember there is no one correct answer for the essay questions, make sure your answer is balanced and developed.